Dust and Breath

DUST AND BREATH

Faith, Health, and
Why the Church Should Care about Both

Kendra G. Hotz & Matthew T. Mathews

WILLIAM B. EERDMANS PUBLISHING COMPANY

GRAND RAPIDS, MICHIGAN / CAMBRIDGE, U.K.

Published 2012 by
Wm. B. Eerdmans Publishing Co.
2140 Oak Industrial Drive N.E., Grand Rapids, Michigan 49505 /
P.O. Box 163, Cambridge CB3 9PU U.K.

Printed in the United States of America

18 17 16 15 14 13 12   7 6 5 4 3 2 1

Library of Congress Cataloging-in-Publication Data

Hotz, Kendra G.
Dust and breath: faith, health, and why the church should care about both /
Kendra G. Hotz & Matthew T. Mathews.
p.   cm.
ISBN 978-0-8028-6779-7 (pbk.: alk. paper)
1. Health — Religious aspects — Christianity. 2. Human body —
Religious aspects — Christianity.   I. Mathews, Matthew T.   II. Title.

BT732.H68   2012

261.8′321 — dc23

2012014981

www.eerdmans.com

Contents

v

126616

Preface

Mel had an obvious black eye. I noticed it as soon as I saw him. There was no doubt in my mind that that was why he was in the clinic. A man in his thirties, he was well dressed and had styled hair.

"So, what happened to you?" I asked jokingly.

"It was really stupid on my part. I tripped on the steps in front of my apartment and hit the trash dumpster."

"It got you pretty good. How much does it hurt?"

"It's mostly my shoulder I'm worried about. I can't raise my arm."

I helped Mel take his shirt off and noted that his shoulder was badly bruised and that he could only move his arm a short distance. The X-ray showed a severely fractured collarbone, and I became worried that the main nerve to his arm might also be damaged.

"I hate to tell you this, but it looks like you might need to have surgery on your shoulder." Mel became silent and started to cry. It was out of character for a man of his age, but I tried to reassure him. "The surgery won't be bad, and you'll be back to normal in six weeks."

"That's not why I'm crying. I don't have any insurance. I've been working at the airport for about a year trying to save up some money. This will take everything I have."

I never cease to be amazed at how this issue can be so close to the surface of people's emotions.

From the journal of Dr. Scott Morris

In 1987 Dr. G. Scott Morris came to Memphis, one of the poorest cities in the nation, to establish a health clinic for the poor. The idea of a clinic for the poor is nothing new, but what Dr. Morris proposed was different. He proposed to open a medical clinic, the Church Health Center, as a ministry of the church, supported by a local congregation whose associate pastor would also serve as the medical director of the clinic. What began as a clinic for the working uninsured in an old house across the street from a congregation with dwindling membership grew into a comprehensive faith and healthcare organization that serves as a nationally recognized model for delivering high-quality care to underserved populations. What began as a ministry in one church grew into an ecumenical and interfaith ministry that draws on tremendously diverse congregations and faith communities. What began as a clinic with one physician has grown into an organization staffed by hundreds of volunteer nurses, physical therapists, social workers, health educators, and physicians and surgeons of every specialty. What began as an effort to heal the sick, one patient at a time, has grown into a comprehensive wellness program that offers not only medical services through a clinic and lab, with referrals for every conceivable specialist, but also a fitness center, health education classes, child life program, and nutrition programming. What began as the church bringing health to the poor has grown into a program for bringing health awareness into congregations.

Without the Church Health Center, someone like Mel, who makes an honest living but who falls through the cracks in our healthcare system, would probably go without care. For him, a simple slip on the stairs could lead to dire poverty or a downward spiral of worsening health caused by not receiving proper care. Because of the Church Health Center, though, Mel was referred to an orthopedic surgeon who keeps free slots on his schedule just for Church Health Center patients. His surgery was success-ful; he was charged only what he was able to afford, and he re-turned to work and to his life. A place like the Church Health Center cannot address all of the social forces that produce a sys-tem in which someone like Mel works but cannot get insurance, but it can and does on a daily basis bring healing and comfort to thousands of people in just his situation. And it does this work as a ministry of the church. It is, after all, the *Church* Health Center.

But why should the church care about health at all? Isn't the work of the church to care for the soul? The book you are now reading began as an effort to articulate the theology embedded in the practices of the Church Health Center; it has grown into a theological reflection on embodiment and the relationship be-tween faith and health. We ask questions about why the church should care about bodies and why medicine should attend to spiritual matters. We explore the biblical and theological founda-tions of a Christian call to minister to bodies — to care for both our own bodies and the bodies of others. We explore what it means that God has created us as bodily beings, how sin distorts our bodies, and how God is working through the church to re-deem us, body and soul. In the life of the church, as we shall see, our own individual wellness is always caught up with healing oth-ers and restoring wholeness in our communities and our world.

We hope that this book will prove useful to three audiences. First, we hope to help those who work in medical institutions such as the Church Health Center as they strive to understand the theological significance of their work. Christian healthcare workers should find here a simple explanation of how their work fits into God's work. Healthcare workers from other religious traditions may also find here a starting point for exploring how their own traditions articulate the link between faith and health. We aim, second, to address congregations who want to think carefully about our lives as embodied creatures and who perhaps hope to initiate their own ministries of health and wellness. Finally, we hope this book will assist seminarians and clergy as they define their own embodied practices and ministries. Obesity levels and the chronic disease rate among clergy are often very high, in large measure because clergy tend to work long hours and neglect their own health even as they offer care to others.[1] We want to convince clergy and those in training for the ministries of the church that good Christian theology demands that they love their own bodies and attend to their own health.

Acknowledgments

This book could not have been produced without the assistance of many people, and we are most grateful for their contributions. We are especially grateful to Dr. Scott Morris for making his journal available to us. Several of the stories in this book come directly from Dr. Morris's journal and display his expertise, compassion, and humility as he treats and learns from his patients. (To preserve confidentiality, all names in these stories have been changed and all identifying details removed or altered.)

We are also grateful to Ann Langston, Butch Odom, and the many staff members of the Church Health Center whose stories

---

1. For instance, a recent report from the Duke University Center for Health Policy that compared United Methodist clergy health to that of the general population in North Carolina found that "male and female clergy combined ages 35 to 64 had significantly higher rates of having ever been told diagnoses of diabetes, arthritis, high blood pressure, and asthma than their NC counterparts." Rae Jean Proeschold-Bell and Sara LeGrand, "High Rates of Obesity and Chronic Disease among United Methodist Clergy," *Obesity* 18 (May 6, 2010): 4. Published online at http://www.nature.com/oby/journal/v18/n9/full/oby2010102a.html.

and perspectives are reflected here. Three individuals — Rev. Stacy Smith, supervisor of Christian formation in wellness at the Church Health Center; John Shorb, editor of *Church Health Reader;* and Rachel Thompson, managing editor of *Church Health Reader* — perceived the need for this project and worked diligently to conceptualize it and bring it to fruition. Without their vision, creativity, and theological acumen this project would not have happened. We owe them a deep debt of gratitude.

In February 2011 eleven wise and patient congregational health promoters participated in an evening of conversation. Their insights and extraordinary accomplishments have inspired and educated us. Some of their stories and insights are included in the book; we wish we could tell them all! We offer our sincere thanks to Brenda Scott Thomas, Nicole Gates, Jenny Hutton, Mia Earl, Sheila Easterling-Smith, Dorothy Hall, Angela Royston, Dorothy Scott, Earl Terrell, Patria Johnson, and Janice Schipp. We also wish to thank Sheridan Smotherman, who organized the conversation and introduced us to the important work of the Congregational Health Promoter program.

We appreciate also the guidance offered by Tom McGowan, associate professor of sociology at Rhodes College, and Arthur Sutherland, retired cardiologist and current advocate for health equity. Leigh DeVries, a recent Rhodes College graduate, contributed helpful background research, identifying important resources on Christian theology and embodiment. Janelle Adams, a current Rhodes College student, served as a summer research fellow in the Child Life Program at the Church Health Center. Her insights about working with children and her stories, some of which appear in this book, have enriched the project. Finally, Rhodes College students who have enrolled in Religious Studies 460 and served as interns at the Church Health Center have, through their thoughtful reflections and penetrating questions, contributed more to this project than they can know.

Chapter One

Dust and Breath

Consider your body. Look at your hands. Feel your pulse. Imagine the bones and cartilage, organs and skin that somehow work together so that you are a living being. Reflect for a moment on the complex levels of coordination between synapses, blood cells, and electrical signals in the brain that allow you to be aware of yourself as a living being. Think also about the bodies of those you love. Remember the smell of your mother's neck when she hugged away your fears. Recall the rich tones of congregational song that helped you perceive the presence of God before you knew how to believe. All of these experiences point us toward an important truth that is remarkably easy to forget and shockingly often denied: we are our bodies. Our most basic sense of ourselves is as bodily beings. And when we love another, we love that person's body: the sound of a friend's voice, the spouse's embrace, the sweetly awkward movements of a child learning to walk.

Sometimes, however, we imagine ourselves as being something other than our bodies. We invent a story about being a noble soul encumbered by a troublesome body and hope for the day when we will be freed from our bodies and fly off to a heavenly home. We imagine that we are our souls and that our bodies are somehow foreign to us. But our experiences of love and fear, of awe and hope tell us that this is fiction, that our home is here, and that these bodies are part and parcel of who we are. If you care for my body, you have cared for me. If I bind up your wounds, I have helped you. If we abuse our bodies, we damage our very selves. We are our bodies.

This is a truth affirmed not only by our experience but also by the Bible.[1] In its most faithful moments the church has woven together its concern for the welfare of human souls with an affirmation that bodily life is what God intends for us, confessing with Psalm 139 that God "formed my inward parts; [and] knit me together in my mother's womb" (v. 13).[2] Your body and the bodies of those you love were created by God to live on this earth and to be resurrected in the new earth. Our experiences as flesh and blood, bone and cartilage, organs and skin are God-given. This biblical story of bodily creation and bodily redemption is the story we must learn to tell again if we are to be faithful disciples of Christ, who came preaching the reign of God, forgiving the sinful, and healing the sick.

Telling the Biblical Story

One of the best places to begin telling the biblical story of bodily creation and bodily redemption is the first two chapters of Genesis. In these chapters we find two different perspectives on creation, which yield complementary insights into our embodi-

---

1. For an excellent treatment of the wide variety of ways in which the Bible affirms the value of the body and grants a central place to healing ministries see Frederick J. Gaiser, *Healing in the Bible: Theological Insights for Christian Ministry* (Grand Rapids: Baker Academic, 2010).

2. All biblical quotations are from the New Revised Standard Version unless otherwise noted.

ment. Chapters 1 and 2 both affirm the fundamental truth that our bodies are God-given and good.

Genesis 2

Let's begin with Genesis 2, which tells us that "the LORD God formed man from the dust of the ground, and breathed into his nostrils the breath of life; and the man became a living being" (Gen. 2:7). Notice first that Genesis tells us that the first person was made out of dust, made from the same elemental stuff as the rest of the world. To be a human being is to be a bodily, material being whose life is intimately and appropriately connected to the material world around us. Our bodies are not accidental accompaniments of our identities; they are instead integral to who we are and gifts of God, rooted in God's creative intentions.

A second thing to notice in Genesis 2 is that God breathed into some of the dust of the earth and that dust became a living person. Neither dust alone nor breath alone makes us who we are. Our bodily identity and spiritual identity are integrated and inseparably united. There is no separate thing called a *soul* that God places inside a different, foreign thing called a *body*. Instead, as God's life-giving breath, soul permeates, saturates, and animates our body. We are ensouled flesh and enfleshed souls — whole selves whose spiritual identity and bodily identity are inextricably interwoven to form the singular fabric of who we are.

Finally, note that Genesis 2 draws attention to three essential features required for human flourishing. First, God places Adam in a garden, in an environment that provides him with the material resources for a healthy life — nutritious food, clean air, unpolluted and fertile soil, and fresh water. The components of this environment create for us a structure or framework in which we live out our lives. By *structure,* we mean a given set of conditions that precedes our choices and actions. Structure refers to the cluster of factors that shape, limit, and frame the particular choices we may eventually make and the actions we may eventually perform. The structures created and willed by God in Genesis 2 are structures that make life-giving, healthy choices and actions possible. If God did not provide the structures of clean air, water, and soil, or nutritious foods, none of us could choose to eat in a healthy manner, enjoy the crisp air during a hike on a cool fall day, or cool ourselves on a hot summer day with a refreshing glass of water or a dip in a mountain stream. Such structures precede our choices and actions, limiting and shaping the opportunities available to us when it comes time to make a choice or act.[3]

Second, God gives Adam a task, to till and keep the soil (v. 14). God provides Adam with meaningful work not as a punishment for sin but as a condition for a good life. He is to use his imagination, intelligence, strong back, and deft hands to learn and to honor the rhythms of nature as he plants and harvests. Of course, we know that this work will become frustrating and difficult after the fall, but in its vision of ideal human life, Genesis 2 affirms the fundamental goodness and necessity of meaningful work for human flourishing.

Third, God recognizes that "it is not good that the man should be alone" (v. 18). God created us as social beings who need companionship and community, and while we have companionship with the rest of creation, we have a special need for human companionship and community. In contrast to the American ideal of rugged individualism, Genesis 2 offers us a vision of shared life lived out in community in which we are, in fact, our brother's and sister's keeper. Our individual lives find

---

3. William C. Cockerham, *Social Causes of Health and Disease* (Malden, MA: Polity Press, 2007), p. 68.

genuine meaning only when we live them out within a dense network of human relationships that bind our lives to those of our
neighbors.

Genesis 1

A careful examination of Genesis 1 also yields important insights into the nature of our bodily life. The first chapter of Genesis provides an account of creation that was especially important
to the people of Judah when they were exiled in Babylon. It tells
the amazing story of God's creative work in a way that contrasts
sharply with the Babylonian creation account found in the
Enuma Elish. The Babylonians believed that the physical world
had come into being as a result of a war among the gods. When
the god Marduk at last defeated Tiamat, the goddess of the deep,
he slaughtered her and formed the world out of her dismem-
bered saltwater body. He formed humans and enlivened them
with the blood of slain rebellious gods. The Babylonians believed that their emperor alone bore the image of Marduk, and
they obeyed the commands their emperor spoke as though he
were a god.

Notice that Genesis 1 insists that the world does not come
into being in the aftermath of some cosmic battle of good
against evil. There is no opposing force — no other god — who
challenges God's creative work. There is no preexisting stuff out
of which God must create that can limit what God makes. God
simply speaks, and what God speaks *becomes.* God creates a
physical world filled with every kind of creature: the magnificent
giant sequoia, the baffling platypus, the playful dolphin, the
ever-curious human. And all of these physical creatures whom
God speaks into being are good. The light and the land, the birds
and the fish, the cattle and the people, all of them are just what

God said they would be; they are individually good and together "very good." Perhaps the most important thing we can learn from contrasting the *Enuma Elish* with Genesis 1 is that in the latter there is no fundamental dualism between good and evil. In the final analysis reality is good because it is made by God; every last speck of it is splendid because it has no source other than God. We should never contrast the goodness of our souls with the evil of our bodies. We should never imagine that there is any force in all of reality that can separate us from God's love (Rom. 8:38-39).

A second important thing to learn from Genesis 1 is that God creates all of humanity in the image of God. The Babylonians would insist that only the emperor bore the divine image, and that, therefore, the emperor had the authority of a god and could use and destroy others with impunity. But the people of Judah could not be cowed by their oppressors because they knew that God's love and justice are mirrored in every human life. They knew that every life is sacred and no life expendable because every human person bears the impression of God's very being. They also knew that every person is created by God with agency. *Agency* refers to our capacity to make choices and to act in ways that shape the direction of our lives and futures and those of our communities. Just as God made a choice to create the world and acts freely to shape it in the way God wants, so too as image-bearers of God we are agents who make choices that shape our world according to our desires.[4] Though we do not have the unlimited power of God, we do exercise some degree of control over our lives and our world. To affirm that every person is created in God's image is to recognize and affirm our agency and ability to

---

4. Throughout this book we will make use of the concepts of *agency* and *structure*. For a treatment of how the tension between agency and structure affects healthcare choices, see Cockerham, *Social Causes,* pp. 49-74.

shape our lives through our choices and actions.[5] Just as there is no fundamental dualism between good and evil, so also in Genesis there is no fundamental hierarchy in human society that grants agency only to some but not others. No human beings by virtue of citizenship or social class, by virtue of gender or sexual orientation, by virtue of age or race, are more worthy than others of a healthful environment, meaningful work, and human companionship as they exercise their agency as image-bearers of God. These essential components of human flourishing are the birthright of every person because all equally share in the image of God.

Third, Genesis 1 teaches us that equality does not mean homogeneity. God made all humanity equally in the image of God, but God did not make all human beings exactly alike. Difference is part of our humanity and a celebrated gift of God. In fact, Genesis 1 draws attention to our diversity at the very point where it affirms our equality as the image of God: "So God created humankind in his image, in the image of God he created them; male and female he created them" (Gen. 1:27). Our bodily differences are crucial to our identities, but not the basis of any kind of hierarchy. We differ by sex and skin color, by height and age, by eye color and foot size. These differences are built into our bodies, written into the fabric of creation, and celebrated as good by a God who intended us to be as different in our bodies as we are alike in God's image.

Fourth, in Genesis 1, notice that human beings are not created on a separate day; rather, they are created on the sixth day, the same day as the other creatures who live on the land. As with these other creatures, the earth is our home and we are to live on

---

5. For an excellent treatment of agency from a theological perspective see Gary Gunderson with Larry Pray, *Leading Causes of Life: Five Fundamentals to Change the Way You Live Your Life* (Nashville: Abingdon Press, 2009), pp. 103-17.

it in a fully embodied way. We thus live out our calling as image-bearers of God in and through our bodies. Thus, Genesis 1 and 2 together emphasize that we human beings are creatures of the earth — made from the dust, spoken into bodily being — who are enlivened by the breath of God and bear the image of God.

Finally, the Genesis 1 creation account does not end with the creation of humanity. The cosmos is complete only on the seventh day when God rests from the labor of creation: "So God blessed the seventh day and hallowed it, because on it God rested from all the work that [God] had done in creation" (Gen. 2:3). On the seventh day, God established a pattern of labor and rest, of creation and recreation, of work and play that would govern the whole world. Just as fields must lie fallow sometimes to remain fertile and productive, so too must human creatures rest and play if they are to work creatively as the image of God. Rest and play are part of our identity as the image of God, and they are essential to our good health.

Dancing the Biblical Story

Thursday the last patient of the day was Ryan, whom I have gotten to know very well over the years. Ryan is now seventy-seven years old and a very lonely man. I think he has always been this way. In the last couple of years his one source of social contact as been our exercise classes. In the past, he fancied himself as a great ballroom dancer, but he has become fairly unsteady on his feet in the last two years. He has often asked me if I thought he would ever be able to dance again, and I have usually said, "Dance as much as you can." Today at the end of our visit, Ryan looked at me and said, "You know, I still love to dance." Knowing how unsteady he is on his feet, I said, "Well, I bet you can still slow dance if you're careful." "Oh, I can still fast dance." Then he paused and with a twinkle in his eye added, "if I lean up against the wall."

From the journal of Dr. Scott Morris

Ryan is a dancer. He has been for a very long time. Dancing is so central to his identity that the first concern he expresses to Dr. Morris is whether he can continue to do it. Dancing is not just what Ryan does; it is also a dimension of who he is. Ryan *is* his body. To name Ryan as a dancer is to name a bodily reality. Dancers move with particular grace, with joy in the precision of form, with delight in the interaction with their partners. When we name Ryan as *dancer,* we name not only that he obviously cannot dance without a body, but also that there is no Ryan apart from his body.

Ryan *is* his body, but he is also *more* than his body. Ryan thinks about his body; he reflects on its changing capacities, imagines dances he might perform and corrections he might make to his steps. He is a self-reflective creature who can think about himself as a creature. We can contrast Ryan's ability to think about his creatureliness to an earthworm, for instance, that simply is its body, but that cannot think about itself as a body, be awed by its role in the process of decomposition, or worry about whether its work is meaningful. The earthworm lives by instinct alone; Ryan lives by questions that puzzle him, hopes that draw him, and plans that guide him.

To be human is to be our bodies but also to be more than our bodies. We cannot be who we are apart from being the bodies that we are, and this means that what happens to our bodies affects our identities. Aging affects Ryan's balance so that he must dance differently and eventually, perhaps, not dance at all. That change, that loss affects his personhood. The shape of his "self" changes and adapts, and sometimes suffers, as the body that is Ryan ages. He still thinks of himself as a dancer, but now when he fast dances, he leans against the wall. The shape of our identities will flow in different directions as the shape of our bodies changes. But because we are more than our bodies, our identities are not wholly *reducible* to what happens to them. Ryan can become unsteady on his feet and still be a dancer. A soldier can lose a leg and still be a parent and a hero. Our bodies affect our identities because even though we are *more* than our bodies, we are not *different* from them.

Genesis 2 teaches us that we are dust and breath; Genesis 1 repeats this truth: we are bodily creatures who bear the image of God. Ryan's story helps us see this biblical truth in our own lives. We *are* our bodies, but are not *reducible* to them; we are *more* than our bodies, but we are not *different* from them. We are dust and breath; creatures who dance and think about ourselves as dancers.

This brief account of the interaction between Ryan and Dr. Morris reveals another important truth as well. Ryan craves contact with other people, and through his relationships with them becomes a richer and more fulfilled person. Ryan was not born into this world a dancer; rather, he became a dancer over time and only through interaction with other dancers and dance partners. Indeed, his ongoing desire to dance, whether fast or slow, is also a desire to live in community and find companionship. Just as part of the very joy of dancing lies in coordinating one's movements with those of another person, so part of the joy of human life resides in immersing ourselves in communities where we find companionship, shared meaning, and fulfillment. Our need for community and companionship is as strong as Ryan's, and it is just as essential to our happiness and health. Indeed, "it is not good that [we] should be alone" (Gen. 2:18).

Health, Companionship, and the Biblical Story

*Late in the day I saw Nora who has already faced a battle
with cancer. Nora is eighty-four years old and had breast
cancer seven years ago. She is a very kind, gentle woman who
faces all challenges in life with a certain consistency. Today
she came with two wrapped presents under her arm. She
handed one to me. "I know it's late, but I brought you your
Christmas present. The other one is for Debbie [a nurse]." I
was touched by her generosity. She went on, "You gave me
such a nice present, and I wanted to let you know how much I
thank you." She was referring to a pair of breast prostheses
that the Church Health Center gave her last summer. Since
her bilateral mastectomy she had been stuffing newspaper
into her bra because she could not afford a pair of artificial
rubber breasts. My cousin, who lives in north Georgia, works
for a company that makes breast prostheses and has offered
to provide them to any of our patients who cannot afford
them. Debbie helped fit Nora and showed her how to use
them. As she handed me the present, Nora went on, "Before
you helped me I was about to have to stop going to church. At
my church during the service there are several times we stop
and hug each other, and I was so embarrassed to have people
press up against me. But now it all feels normal. I'm so proud
and I thank you for it." I had not thought that a poor eighty-
four-year-old woman would care that much about such a
thing. I was wrong.*

From the journal of Dr. Scott Morris

Dr. Morris's encounter with Nora illuminates some important
dimensions of how our view of health grows out of a biblical understanding of the body. Specifically it highlights three impor-

tant dimensions of a biblical, holistic vision of health. First, health means more than the absence of disease. Second, health is a dynamic concept. And third, health includes social engagement and companionship.

First, Nora's story helps shed light on what we mean by *health* and *wellness*. When we hear the phrase *healthy person* we often imagine a person who is free of disease. We equate health with the absence of illness. But as Dr. Morris reminds us, "being disease free does not make you healthy. . . . Wellness embraces the joy of living then acts in a way that allows for thriving in happiness, love, and closeness to God."[6] Healthcare, accordingly, is designed to eliminate disease from the body. When we use the term in this way, we think of Nora as healthy once the cancer has been removed from her body, but her story shows us that this definition of health is too narrow. While health certainly encompasses the absence of disease, when our understanding of health is rooted in a biblical view of the body we can recognize it as a far more comprehensive concept.

Rather than thinking of health as the absence of disease, the Bible encourages us to think of health as the presence of the conditions necessary for us to flourish, to become what God intends for us. For Nora, *health* meant not simply the elimination of cancer cells, but also the provision of prostheses and guidance in their use so that she might fully participate in her community of faith without fear of embarrassment or self-consciousness.

Second, Nora's story reveals that a biblical vision of health is also dynamic. Our understanding of health must embrace changes in our bodies across our lifetimes. Our bodies, and therefore our identities, change as we age, when we lose or gain

---

6. Scott Morris with Susan Martins Miller, *Healthcare You Can Live With: Discover Wholeness in Body and Spirit* (Uhrichsville, OH: Barbour Publishing, 2011), p. 81.

weight, when we suffer injury or illness, when we begin to exercise, and when we become pregnant and give birth. Healthcare must accommodate this dynamic dimension of health. Our "ideal body," the one medicine seeks to heal and restore, is not the one we had at twenty years of age. It is the body that enables us to engage in meaningful work and relationships at every stage of life. Healthcare must be adaptive and responsive not only to the physiological changes that accompany aging, but also to the environmental, vocational, and social adaptations. Given the dynamic nature of health and the adaptive responsibility of healthcare, we must recognize that healing ministries have work to do even when ill, injured, and aging persons cannot be fully restored. Nora needs prosthetic breasts and the confidence to hug others. The HIV-positive woman needs continuing drug therapy and social engagement. The diabetic man who has suffered an amputation needs meaningful work. Those struggling to maintain a healthy body weight need supportive communities. And we all need opportunities to reflect on how what happens to our bodies shapes the persons we are becoming. There is no singular, ideal state of health. What it means for us to be healthy will be as varied as the persons God calls us to be.

Third, Nora's story reminds us that we were made for companionship. Recall from our look at Genesis 2 that God provided humanity with the conditions for a good life: a healthful environment, meaningful work, and companionship. Here we focus on the dimension of companionship and social engagement as a condition of health. Our lives are meant to be woven into a fabric of meaningful relationships. We know that when we are woven into such relationships, our health is better and our lives longer.[7] Families, friends, congregations, and coworkers create bonds of mutual responsibility that fill our days with challenges

7. Cockerham, *Social Causes,* p. 169.

and delight. Nora's story demonstrates this perfectly. Her health is not established simply by the elimination of cancer; her health is restored only when she is able to participate fully once again in the life of her congregation, when she is able to hug others without feeling self-conscious about doing so. Healthcare must seek to restore people to good relationships, and that includes the relationship between the recipient and the provider of healthcare. It is important that Nora not simply receive from but also give to Dr. Morris and Debbie. She gives not only Christmas gifts but also her kind, gentle presence. Dr. Morris enjoys his time with Nora. He listens to and learns from her. She is not, to him, "the cancer patient in room four." She is Nora: he knows her name; he knows her story. His role in restoring her health has not left her in the role of passive recipient; it has enabled her once again to enter the world as an active agent who both gives and receives.

Health, Environment, and the Biblical Story

Kelsey and Malaya are sisters, ages four and six, who participate in the Child Life Program at the Church Health Center's Wellness Campus. On Wednesday, we spent nearly half an hour together in the play kitchen, and by the end of that time, the play kitchen was a disaster. Before moving on to the next game, I told them that we were going to play something really fun, a game called "Sort the Kitchen." Usually, this "game" works well, with children and myself pretending to work at a grocery store where we are sorting out food items by category and stocking them on the shelves for shoppers. With Kelsey and Malaya, however, the game became a real challenge. I began the game by calling out the category of "fruit," instructing each girl to bring me as much fruit as she could as fast as she could. Instead of fruit, however, they brought me ham, celery, eggs, and spaghetti. Realizing their confusion, I slowed things down to talk about what fruit is. I pointed out different examples of fruit in the kitchen. When I felt as if everything had been sufficiently explained, we returned to the game. This time when I called out "fruit," six-year-old Malaya came to me with a box for apple pie and told me proudly, "This is the fruit we eat at home!"

From the field observation notes of Janelle Adams,
Rhodes College research fellow

Good health allows us to live out our God-given identities. It encompasses our whole persons as dust and breath creatures. Comprehensive healthcare, therefore, must seek not only to remove disease but also to create conditions or structures that allow for holistic health. The story of Kelsey and Malaya reminds us that healthcare must address the environmental conditions that are necessary for healthful living and seek to ameliorate conditions that contribute to disease and disability. To be healthy, we need to live in places where clean water is available and the air is breathable. But we also need to live in communities that are safe so that people can walk and exercise in their neighborhoods without having to drive to expensive "health clubs" and where children can play outdoors. We need to live in homes free of lead-based paint. We need access to affordable, nutritious foods. While there are numerous factors that contribute to a healthful environment, the story of Kelsey and Malaya focuses our attention on one crucial component: access to fresh, natural food.

What has happened when children cannot identify fruit on their own? What is going on when, even after instruction, their closest association with an apple is a commercially produced, boxed apple pie? Kelsey and Malaya are likely growing up in a "food desert," a place where calories are abundant but nutrition is scarce. Many of our nation's urban areas include these so-called "food deserts," neighborhoods that have no source for natural, raw, whole foods.[8] Instead, these neighborhoods are filled with fast food restaurants, liquor stores, and convenience stores selling highly processed junk "food." Obtaining fresh produce in such neighborhoods is expensive and inconvenient. You may be able to purchase an inexpensive, fried "apple" pie at a nearby fast food chain, but you would be hard pressed to find an actual apple anywhere.

When we hear the story of Kelsey and Malaya, we may be tempted to make judgments about the poor nutrition choices that they or their parents make. We may wish to exhort them to exercise their God-given agency in better ways by choosing healthy food over junk food. But when we think about the existence of the food desert, we realize that something more is going on, that providing a healthful environment involves more than having the individual willpower to choose an apple over an apple pie. Kelsey and Malaya's agency has already been severely curtailed by a structure that does not allow for good choices. In a food desert, there are no apples or cherries available, so Kelsey and Malaya can only choose between equally unhealthy apple pies and cherry pies. They do not have the chance to choose healthy fruit, so their choices are simply between equally unhealthy processed food options. In the words of one sociologist, their "life choices" are significantly determined by their "life chances."[9] "Life chances," of course, do not happen by chance;

8. For more information on food deserts see the National Research Council, *The Public Health Effects of Food Deserts* (Washington, DC: The National Academies Press, 2009). Mark Winne offers a compelling account of what leads to food deserts and how to change these circumstances in *Closing the Food Gap: Resetting the Table in the Land of Plenty* (Boston: Beacon Press, 2008).

9. Cockerham, *Social Causes,* p. 59.

we human beings construct the kinds of chances we can have through our collective social, political, and economic policies. The world given to us by God presents us with choices between apples and oranges, bananas and cherries. The world we construct through the complex interplay of our economic system, zoning laws, and policies for public transportation, for example, creates chances for some of us to choose among good foods or between good foods and junk foods; but those same realities severely restrict the chances for those living in a food desert, so that their only choice is between equally unhealthy varieties of junk food. The structures we live in provide us with the chances within which we exercise our agency as we make choices.

A biblical commitment to the goodness of the body and to the conditions for health will draw us far beyond the walls of hospitals and doctors' offices into the particular communities in which we live. The conditions for health emerge through careful, communal planning involving everything from zoning laws to water policy, from code enforcement to policing philosophies, and this means that our commitment to health will draw us into the realm of structural and social analysis and public planning. All of us make our choices within an inherited set of structures that determine the nature and scope of the options from which we choose. It is not enough merely to exhort Malaya, Kelsey, and their parents to make better choices. We must work to create a better set of structures since doing so is the only way for their choices to have meaningful health outcomes for their lives. Concern for health and healthcare will draw us into the world of policymaking and active participation in the civic and political processes that produce neighborhoods in which the environmental conditions for health take hold and flourish.

Health, Vocation, and the Biblical Story

Working with Hadley at the sand station today, I noticed how meticulous she was in her play. Time after time she used the hand brush to scoop the sand into a pile until literally almost every last grain was where she wanted it to be. When I mentioned something about how careful she was being, she paused and thought for a minute. At last she confided that she had never been to the beach: "I know there are beaches because Hawaii is the beach. And I think if I ever went to the beach I would want to take care of it. Yes, I would want to take care of it so that everybody could come see it, and not just some people."

In the afternoon the only other child I had the opportunity to work with was a two-year-old named Adalae. We built with blocks for a while, until she realized that these blocks had pictures on all sides that could form a larger picture if placed together correctly. Thrilled about this, she knocked over her tower and started to lay out the blocks, though in an order that in no way created the desired scene. Completely unconcerned about this fact, she turned to me and solemnly confided, "This is going to be beautiful!"

From the field observation notes of Janelle Adams,
Rhodes College research fellow

When God created human beings, God not only placed them in a healthful environment but also gave them meaningful work to do. Therefore, our understanding of health must be connected to the tasks that God has created and called us to do. Soundness of body and faithfulness to God's calling are intimately connected. Health enables us to engage in the meaningful work that is an essential dimension of a good life. And engaging in good work contributes to our health. Just as being sick makes us unable to work, so also being unable to work can make us sick. Researchers have shown a consistent link between the stresses of unemployment and increased chances of disease and death.[10] Good health and good work go together both in the Garden of Eden and in the places where we live.

But we must be careful here that when we talk about "meaningful work" we do not reduce its meaning to "wage-earning work." Certainly good health will enable us to engage in a livelihood that will provide for our material needs. But the good work to which God calls us includes more than income-generating work. In the Christian tradition, we have used the term *vocation* to refer broadly to *all* the tasks and activities to which God calls us, regardless of whether they generate income. We may be called to parenthood, to volunteer in our churches, to create works of art, to serve our communities as sanitation workers, fire fighters, entrepreneurs, or librarians. A holistic understanding of health, then, will recognize that our bodies must be fit to the tasks to which God calls us. Even when our bodies are disabled by injury, disease, or old age, we can be healthy so long as we are able to engage in the tasks of our vocation.

When we hear the term *vocation,* most of us think of the work we do as adults. But if vocation refers more broadly to all the ways we do the things God calls us to do, then we must broaden the scope of vocation to include a place for children. Recognizing children, too, as image-bearers of God who have a vocation is part of acknowledging the dynamic character of health. *Health* does not name the idealized body of the young adult in peak physical condition. It also encompasses the changes in our bodies from

10. See "Not Just a Paycheck" in the series *Unnatural Causes . . . Is Inequality Making Us Sick?* (San Francisco: California Newsreel, 2008), transcript p. 8. Published online at http://www.unnaturalcauses.org/assets/uploads/file/UC_Transcript_7.pdf.

infancy into childhood and on to adulthood and old age. To be sure, a child's vocation is not one of wage-earning work. At the heart of children's vocation is *play*. This may sound odd to us as adults, but children are created by God to be playful, to explore their world with imagination, freedom, and make-believe. Play is work for children; when they do it, they are participating in God's intention for their lives. Play is thus not frivolous activity. In play, children are exercising their imaginations as well as their bodies, stretching and exploring the ways in which the world works. In play, children often pretend or "practice" at adulthood, and such play is an essential part of the human maturation process and contributes to a healthy body, mind, and spirit. Consider Hadley, who is busily playing in the sand, meticulously moving and arranging it into the kind of place that she imagines a beach to be. Consider Adalae, who is arranging blocks and exploring newly discovered images on them. Consider both children as they stretch their imaginations, cultivate an other-orientedness that delights in creating a beautiful block house or tropical beach for all to enjoy. With both hands and toy tools, Hadley is exercising her imagination about a place she's never been, and in doing so she is trying to sculpt a beautiful world for all people who will eventually visit her imaginary tropical beach. It is the same with Adalae as she suddenly discovers new ways of arranging the blocks and tries to do so in a way that others will find beautiful. This "work" is cultivating features of good health. Hadley and Adalae are stretching their imaginations and exploring worlds that could be but are not yet available to them. They are learning to affirm that the world as given to them is not necessarily the world they must accept. Hadley can move sand and sculpt a different world; Adalae can rearrange the blocks to create a more beautiful building. Play is cultivating their sense of agency and contributing to the self-confidence and the sense of new possibilities that are essential to a meaningful, healthy life.

When we cannot "move sand" or "rearrange the blocks," so to speak, and explore new ways of arranging the features of our world in life-giving ways, we easily sink into hopelessness, despair, and fatalism. Children who grow up without play risk an underdevelopment of agency and imagination, and it is hard for them to think creatively about the kind of life they want for themselves. An essential feature of children's health and vocation, then, involves allowing and encouraging them to play, for it is in play that children exercise body, mind, and spirit as part of their vocation before God and in so doing prepare themselves for rich adult lives. The importance of play, though, is not restricted to children. Adults know well the sense of despair that can accompany unemployment, but often forget that they, too, need time for play, time for the free range of the imagination. Adult play as much as the play of children is crucial for allowing us to envision a better world and to reimagine our role in it. We need to lose ourselves in a good book, shout for joy when our team scores a goal, and stroll peacefully through expansive city parks.

Hadley and Adalae have a second lesson to teach us as well. Notice that each of them delights in creating beauty that others might enjoy. For Hadley, her efforts in the sand are about creating and maintaining a beautiful tropical beach for all people to enjoy, and for Adalae there is the moment of discovery in which she sees the images stamped on the blocks and declares, "This is going to be *beautiful!*" Both girls point to an important theological insight about vocation in a consumerist culture, an insight that has important implications for our health. The consumerist culture in which we live encourages us to consume and discard things at will, whether fast food, fast cars, or larger and larger houses. In the culture of consumerism, we come to define ourselves by what and how much we consume.[11] Consumerism sub-

11. Cockerham, *Social Causes,* p. 51.

tly redefines the value of work, threatening to strip it of its meaning as part of our vocation. Many of us work so that we can spend and consume, but such spending and consuming carries us far beyond the essentials of a good life. Our spending and consuming are often excessive and become the key source of our identity and meaning in life. We pursue ever greater amounts of wealth, so that we can add more square footage to our homes, buy larger fuel-inefficient vehicles, and fill our homes with more and more stuff. Somehow we come to believe that these markers of consumer prosperity will bring happiness and wholeness to our lives.

Consumerism is a form of idolatry that invests finite things with ultimate value and meaning and seeks from them the ultimate peace, security, and fulfillment that only God can give. This idolatry affects our health at both the individual and the social level — it affects both our agency and the structures within which we exercise that agency. At the level of individual agency, consumerism leads us to rearrange the world around ourselves. We work longer hours, often forgoing leisure time with our children and spouses so that we can increase our spending power in that ever-elusive search for a meaningful life through endless consumption. A long workday in a sedentary job compromises our physical fitness, and isolation from our friends and families compromises our mental health.

But consumerism also affects our health as a society by distorting the structures that enable or constrain agency. It does so for two reasons. First, consumerism leads us to measure the value of everything, including healthcare, in terms of dollars. We come to believe that "you get what you pay for," and that every social good — whether widgets or organ transplants, automobiles or immunizations — should be available for purchase. The wealthy somehow deserve not only larger cars and homes, but also better healthcare. Second, consumerism affects our health at the social level because it introduces class distinctions that have very real bodily consequences. Social inequality "gets under the skin" and disrupts our health.[12]

Hadley and Adalae can remind us of a key feature of vocation; namely, that when we engage in our vocations we are engaging in God's work and seeking to be partners in God's restoration of the world after the pattern of God's reign. In vocation, we work, but not primarily to consume. In vocation, we work to contribute to the common good, to create for others a better and healthier world. In vocation, we shape sand into beaches that all may enjoy and build block-buildings that provide homes and neighborhoods that are beautiful and available for all. Like Hadley and Adalae, Christians work to create a beautiful world for others as part of the great redemptive beautification project of God's coming reign.

Sabbath

In the previous three sections, we have seen how the story of the Garden of Eden reminds us that companionship, a healthful environment, and meaningful work are important components of good health. In this section we turn to the account of creation in Genesis 1 to remember that rest also is part of God's intention for creation and is crucial for our well-being. In the first creation story of Genesis, we are told that on the seventh day God rested. This divine sabbath forms the basis of the fourth commandment: "Remember the sabbath day, and keep it holy. Six days you shall labor and do all your work. But the seventh day is a sabbath

12. Richard Wilkinson and Kate Pickett, *The Spirit Level: Why Greater Equality Makes Societies Stronger* (New York: Bloomsbury Press, 2009), p. 31. We will explore the idea that social inequalities produce health disparities in more detail in the next chapter.

to the LORD your God; you shall not do any work. . . . For in six days the LORD made heaven and earth, the sea, and all that is in them, but rested the seventh day; therefore, the LORD blessed the sabbath day and consecrated it" (Exod. 20:8-11). The fourth commandment, to honor the Sabbath, is grounded in the rhythm and structure of creation itself. Just as God rests after six days of work, so human beings are commanded to honor our need for rest, worship, and the revitalization of our bodies, minds, and spirits that comes with sabbath.

The church has sometimes focused its understanding of sabbath rather narrowly. We have insisted that businesses be closed on Sunday, that we do not work on Sunday, and even that children not be allowed to ride their bicycles or play outdoors. But Scripture calls us toward sabbath as a deeper and more far-reaching principle than this. As Jesus himself taught us when he allowed his disciples to engage in work by plucking heads of grain for food on the sabbath and by declaring, "The sabbath was made for humankind, and not humankind for the sabbath," sabbath is not about restricting in legalistic fashion this or that single behavior (Mark 2:27). The real significance of sabbath lies in recognizing that structured into our very creatureliness and that of the entire creation is a divinely created rhythm of work and rest that must be honored in our lives if we are to be healthy. Honoring sabbath means becoming intentional about cultivating a total life pattern that balances work and rest. Rest is just as essential to good health as work is. Sabbath, therefore, embraces more than mere Sunday observance; it embraces and affirms all those ways in which we take time to reground ourselves in the life-giving rhythms of creation and find there refreshment, rejuvenation, and new life. Sabbath includes time off from work, vacations on Hadley's tropical beach, enjoyment of the arts, and enjoyment of sports and a myriad of other leisure activities. Such forms of sabbath reground us in the grace-filled, life-giving rhythm established by God and by so doing contribute to health in body, mind, and spirit.

In our contemporary world, we often confront two distinct threats to sabbath. First, many of us, caught as we are on the treadmill of consumerism, simply refuse to take a sabbath rest. We work ten- or twelve-hour days, go into the office on Saturday and maybe Sunday afternoon to "get more done." We sacrifice time with our families, churches, and neighbors in the elusive quest to make more money so that we can consume more and hopefully find fulfillment and happiness. When we choose a rhythm of life that neglects sabbath, it comes at the cost of our health. We do not exercise our bodies; we cheat our children and spouses of the time necessary for a rich family life, and we risk burn-out that destroys our spirits as well as our bodies. In such situations, sabbath calls us to exercise agency, to evaluate the pattern of choices we have made as well as the values that inform them, seeking to rediscover that balanced rhythm of work and rest.

While for some of us failure at sabbath is a choice pressed upon us by consumerism, for others of us it is a necessity forced upon us by an economic system that includes jobs that do not pay a living wage or provide benefits to employees. As a result, some of us must scramble to hold down two or more jobs just to keep food on the table and clothes on our backs. In this situation, we do not observe sabbath because we cannot, because economic circumstances and social structures force us to choose between observing the sabbath and surviving. These tragic conditions create the world of the working poor, the world of those who work long hours each week and still find themselves trapped in poverty, unable to observe sabbath if they or their children are to eat, be clothed, or make it to school each day. The structures that create the world of the working poor undermine the possibility of sabbath and by so doing uproot us from the divine rhythm of work and rest that is essential to good health. In this world, the choice is not between work and sabbath, but between work and nothingness; it is another severely constrained choice between cherry pie and apple pie. The fresh fruit of sabbath is not available.

Enacting the Biblical Story

"Ministry in the church is more than the preaching part."
"For so long we thought we had the spiritual part down pat, and we thought what was wrong with us could be fixed with just a prayer."

From a conversation with
Congregational Health Promoters

A careful reading of the creation stories in Genesis reveals that human beings are not souls encumbered with bodies. We are bodies. Our spiritual identity and our physical identity cannot be separated. They are inseparably interwoven with one another. We are dust made alive by the breath of God. Because the church is not called to minister to souls or to bodies, but to whole persons, the Church Health Center offers nine-week classes so that members of local congregations can come and be trained in some basic areas of healthcare. At the end of the nine-week program participants are certified as Congregational Health Promoters, and they are empowered to return to their congregations with information about nutrition and diabetes, ready to teach the symptoms of a stroke, and eager to help members of their congregations connect with healthcare resources in the community. Too often in the Christian tradition we have drawn a clear but false distinction between body and soul and assigned to the church the ministry of souls and to medicine the ministry of the body. But the Bible demands that the church must care about the body and medicine must care about more than the body. The Congregational Health Promoters help to bridge that gap, but they report that "it can be hard to get people to believe they need to care about their bodies."

The church must care about the body. When the church embraces its ministry to whole persons, it will become intentional in creating programs and ministries that encourage the redemption of the whole person. Sometimes these ministries will be clearly related to the bodies of congregation members: there will be exercise classes and nutrition education, the potluck will include fresh produce, there will be counseling available for those suffering addictions. Other times congregations will address health concerns in the broader community: the building will be open for twelve-step program meetings; the congregation will sponsor free health clinics and forums on community planning; there will be blood drives and educational events. Congregations might host neighborhood association meetings and meetings with community leaders to discuss ways to nurture those qualities of environment that contribute to health. Broadening the ministry of the church so that it addresses whole persons will thus involve cultivating not merely personal faith and private morality but also a strong sense of citizenship and civic responsibility anchored in faith and capable of shaping the kinds of neighborhoods we live in and the kinds of communities we become.

If the church has sometimes been tempted to limit its ministry to souls apart from bodies, then healthcare has sometimes been tempted to limit its work to bodies apart from souls. Augustus White, a professor at Harvard University Medical School, explains that "there is a culture of medicine that conditions physicians to focus on the patient's physiological symptoms and biomedical indications and discourages them from taking into account the social context. . . . Doctors learn to value 'what medicine cares about' and to discount the human side." As they adopt the culture and values of the medical establishment, physicians take on the "medical gaze."[13] Medicine, in other words, looks only at the body, and does not "care about" the spirits that enliven the flesh they treat.

But if, as Genesis teaches, human personhood consists in the marvelous, mysterious union of body and soul, medicine must aim not merely at the healing of bodies but at the healing of whole persons. Jesus acknowledged the importance of the "human side" when he healed the woman with the issue of blood (Mark 5:25-34). She reached out from the crowd to touch the hem of his robe and was made well. Jesus could have continued on his way without stopping to identify her. He was, after all, on his way to an emergency call to heal Jairus's daughter. The "medical gaze" was all the woman wanted, the simple touch to heal her body. But Jesus rejected the medical gaze when he stopped in his tracks and asked, "Who touched me?" It mattered to him that he should know the ones he healed.

Jesus the great physician can become the model for our own healthcare providers. When we recognize that *health* refers not merely to the absence of disease but instead to the presence of all those conditions of environment, social relationships, and vocation that lead to human flourishing, we must expand our understanding of the nature and function of healthcare so that it recognizes and honors the undeniable ways that the spiritual and bodily dimensions of our lives are woven together. White calls for a new, "patient-centered" model of medicine that en-

---

13. Augustus A. White III, *Seeing Patients: Unconscious Bias in Healthcare* (Cambridge, MA: Harvard University Press, 2011), p. 221. White borrows this analysis and the term "medical gaze" from medical anthropologist Mary-Jo Good.

courages healthcare workers to "care about" more than their patients' bodies.[14] When healthcare workers become "patient-centered" they set aside the medical gaze and take up the vision of Christ. They come to know their patients as full persons and to attend to multiple dimensions of their wellness. The vision of Christ calls us always to remain aware that human bodies are not machines. We can replace the tires on our car without concern for its spiritual health. But we cannot touch bodies, draw blood, listen to hearts, perform surgeries, prescribe drugs, or assist with physical therapy without affecting the "self" who is that body. Healthcare does not seek to heal bodies for their own sake; rather, it seeks to heal bodies in pursuit of healthy and whole personhood.

Furthermore, just as healthcare providers cannot touch their patients' bodies without affecting their personhood, so also those providers cannot touch their patients' bodies without being affected themselves. If patients are to be givers as well as receivers, then doctors, nurses, and other providers must be receivers as well as givers of care. Nurturing health in patients involves nurturing their capacity for agency and honoring it as essential to their full personhood. Patients, those who are acted upon, are also always agents whose presence acts upon those who care for them. Healthcare providers know that it is vital to develop a professional presence in order to provide appropriate care to patients, but this "professional distance" should never become utter detachment lest patients be reduced to widgets on an assembly line, to machines, or to "the cancer in room four." If human beings are "fearfully and wonderfully made," we must provide healthcare in a manner befitting the sacred mystery of personhood.

As we have seen throughout this chapter, a biblical vision of

14. White, *Seeing Patients*, p. 228.

human personhood requires that we see human beings as whole beings, ensouled flesh and enfleshed souls whose spiritual and bodily life are integrally related to one another. When we speak of *health,* therefore, we must do so in ways that honor this fundamental insight, and we do this best by broadening our definition of health beyond the mere absence of disease. Health refers to the presence of a comprehensive set of conditions that promote human flourishing and are anchored in our environmental, social, and vocational lives. This biblical understanding of human personhood and health has implications for both the church and medicine. For the church, it means discovering and exploring concretely the way in which the gospel is good news for our bodies. For healthcare it means discovering and exploring concretely the way in which healing is gospel for our souls.

Chapter Two

Finitude and Sin:
Returning to Dust and Coming Undone

A biblical understanding of human personhood affirms that we are bodily beings and that it is good to be so. Genesis insists that God alone creates the world and that, therefore, there is no separate source of reality at war with God. We do not live in a divided cosmos where forces of evil are arrayed against the forces of God. We and all creatures are called into being by an infinitely good and loving God who is the source of everything that exists and the only foundation of reality. We do not choose sides in some cosmic battle between the gods of good and evil. As Paul proclaims, in God "we live and move and have our being" (Acts 17:28). If we do not live in God, then we do not live at all. If we do not have our being in God, then we are nothing.

The insistence in Genesis that there is no fundamental dualism of good and evil, though, seems to be in conflict with our ordinary experience of the world. We know that we experience profound suffering, that our world is filled with evil, and that our lives are marred by sin. And we know that sin and evil have very real consequences for our bodily lives. In this chapter we will explore a biblical account of sin and evil and its implications for the church's ministries of health and wellness. When we return to consider Genesis 1–3, we discover two key insights related to sin and evil that bear directly on our understanding of personhood and health. The first is that we are creatures; the second is that we are sinful. Let's begin by reflecting on our creatureliness.

Returning to Dust: Being a Creature

Glenn has always been one of my favorite patients. He is now ninety-two years old, blind from glaucoma, and lives with his niece. When he first started coming to see me twelve years ago, he still lived on his own little farm and worked it every day. When he first visited me it had been more than twenty years since he had seen a doctor, so I knew to take his complaint seriously. His concern was that he was suffering from shortness of breath. He did not smoke, and his chest X-ray and lung function were normal, so I began to check to see if there was a problem with his heart. His ECG was normal, and he did well on a treadmill test, especially considering that he was eighty years old at the time. After several visits and a long list of tests turning up normal, I questioned him one more time about his shortness of breath.

"Now, Glenn, when exactly do you get short of breath?"
"I get out of breath when I'm working on my new barn."
"Is it when you do any kind of work on the barn?"
"No, only when I'm pushing my wheelbarrow."
"So, what are you carrying in the wheelbarrow?"
"Concrete."

After doing thousands of dollars of tests, I concluded that it was normal for an eighty-year-old man to get short of breath while carrying concrete in a wheelbarrow, but I never truly convinced him of that.

From the journal of Dr. Scott Morris

Glenn's story points us to one of the most basic truths that Genesis teaches us: we are creatures. To be a creature means that we are finite. We are born; we grow old; our bodies change and sometimes falter; even the most vigorous among us, the eighty-year-old who can still work a farm and push a wheelbarrow filled with concrete, will age and die. We come from nothing and are held in existence by forces beyond our control. Our lives develop according to conditions and purposes that are ultimately rooted not in ourselves but in the wisdom and mystery of God. To be creatures means that we are limited, and this limitation encompasses both the spiritual and bodily dimensions of who we are. Our knowledge is limited. Our capacity to shape our future is limited; from our ancestors we inherit genetic materials that exert great influence over the shape of our bodies, the color of our skin, hair, and eyes, and the types of illnesses we may be prone to experience. We are born at a time and in an age that we do not choose, and the nature and number of our days are measured out for us by God. Much of who we are is simply given to us rather than chosen or controlled by us, and while we make decisions, we do so within the framework of the limitations placed on us by God and nature.

Our finitude, however, is not a curse but a gift of God. Genesis teaches that it is good to be a creature with all the attendant limitations that accompany it. Embracing the goodness of our finitude and creatureliness is important for thinking about our health. Accepting and celebrating our creatureliness means recognizing that our lives have beginnings, middles, and ends, and that in each of these seasons our bodies manifest their goodness in different ways. When we speak of a "healthy person," our understanding must be shaped by this reality. A healthy sixteen-year-old and a healthy eighty-year-old will be healthy in different ways. Embracing our finitude also means accepting and celebrating our bodily differences not only over time, but also across the spectrum of human diversity. We will differ in skin color and height, in body shape and vocal tone. Just as we need not idealize the perfectly fit youthful body as the model for health, so also we need not imagine that there is a single bodily norm that perfectly enfleshes human beauty. For many years, medical researchers made the mistake of assuming that the white, male body could stand in for all human bodies. New drugs and treatments had only to be tested on such bodies, and they could be declared safe and effective for the whole human community. Ailments that tended to affect primarily women were likely to be dismissed as existing "only in her head" and those that affected racial minorities were less likely to take center stage in research.[1]

Healthcare must be adaptive and responsive to the rhythms, patterns, and limitations of the human life cycle, honoring the divinely given limitations placed on our lives by God. Healthcare should not ignore our finitude or aim to overcome it, and neither should it aim to conform all bodies to a single standard of health and beauty. Instead, healthcare should aim to assist us as we live out our finitude in healthy ways. Given the scope and pace of scientific development and medical technology, we must be especially mindful of this truth. We must not make of medicine a god, asking it to transform us into immortals or to overcome our every limitation. For instance, while we may have the technological and medical capacity to perform extraordinary interventions to promote health, we must be careful that such extraordinary measures are not used inappropriately to extend life beyond its appointed end. Likewise, in the difficult struggle with infertility, we might ask ourselves at what point adoption is a more favor-

1. Augustus White, for instance, explains that doctors "were more likely to believe that heart problems of women who reported stress were due to psychological causes, whereas men who talked about stress were considered more likely to have organic heart disease." *Seeing Patients: Unconscious Bias in Health Care* (Cambridge, MA: Harvard University Press, 2011), p. 238.

able option than remaining on an accelerating treadmill of ever more invasive and costly medical solutions.

While our finitude is good, it is not always easy. Aging bodies bring discomfort, frustration, and a curtailment of life's activities. Infertility often brings emotional pain and can severely strain the lives of couples spiritually, bodily, socially, and financially. And so while finitude is good, it is also sometimes tragic. It is good to be a creature, though being a creature means being limited, vulnerable, and dependent. Those very limitations, vulnerabilities, and dependencies mean that we do not always reach our goals, that we are sometimes wounded by the world that sustains us, and that eventually our lives end. Our good finitude, in other words, can be painful. This inevitable intertwining of goodness and pain, of beauty and sorrow, constitutes the tragic dimension of our lives as creatures.

In *Caring Cultures: How Congregations Respond to the Sick,* Susan Dunlap explores illness as part of the tragic dimension of our finitude and explains that "illness brings many deep human desires . . . to the fore."[2] She outlines three desires that are challenged by illness. First, every person has a deep desire for safety.[3] We sense that the world is a hospitable place for us. We know that our lives are sustained by the air we breathe and by the food that springs up from rich soil, and that our days are enriched by the immense beauty of the world. Of course, sometimes the creation is also a dangerous place for us, and so we seek safety from the elements in the homes we live in, and we fortify ourselves against scarcity by storing up goods. We long for safety and build up social structures to provide it. But illness disrupts our sense that the world is hospitable and defies our efforts to provide se-

2. Susan J. Dunlap, *Caring Cultures: How Congregations Respond to the Sick* (Waco: Baylor University Press, 2009), p. 11.
3. Dunlap, *Caring Cultures,* p. 191.

curity for ourselves. Diseases creep into our bodies in spite of the goodness of the world and in spite of our own best efforts. Illness leaves us with a shaken sense of safety. Even though Glenn does not suffer from an illness, he is feeling acutely the reduced strength and stamina that are a natural part of the aging process, and as a man who has prided himself on self-reliance, hard work, and independence, he likely senses acutely the possibility that he is losing his capacity to do those things that have sustained him as an independent adult for most of his life. Much of Glenn's security in life has come at his own hands, so fear of losing his capacity for self-reliance and independence is a powerful factor that attends his changing health.

Second, we have a deep desire for relationship that is part of our finitude.[4] We long for the give-and-take of human connection. We were made for companionship and social interaction. We take deep delight in helping each other, in sharing meals and conversation, and in working and playing together. In our best relationships there is a mutuality that destroys hierarchy, and there is a hospitality that gives without counting the cost and receives without being burdened by obligation. But illness disrupts our relationships in many ways. "The person who is sick is often not able to return empathy or acts of kindness or to do daily chores."[5] Those who are seriously ill may no longer be able to work alongside others or even to enjoy common meals. When we are sick we may need to receive far more that we are able to give, and this can lead to a sense of guilt. As we age, we may become increasingly dependent on others and begin to feel that the egalitarianism that is the hallmark of most adult relationships is slowly eroding and being replaced with a hierarchy of caregiver and care-receiver. Finally, sometimes our relationships

4. Dunlap, *Caring Cultures,* p. 191.
5. Dunlap, *Caring Cultures,* p. 191.

are disrupted because as illness wears away our bodily integrity or mental acuity, or as death approaches, friends and loved ones may become frightened or overwhelmed and begin to distance themselves. The sick often find themselves isolated and lonely. Illness may leave us with diminished relationships. Consider Glenn once again. His relationship with his niece has surely changed. When they were both younger, Glenn likely related to her as an adult relates to a child. He was part of that circle of caregivers and protectors that ensured that she grew into a healthy, self-reliant adult. Now in his later years, their relationship is largely different. Glenn lives with and relies on his niece for his well-being. She is now his caregiver in ways that represent an awkward inversion of the way things once were. As he ages, Glenn will likely become even more dependent on his niece and may worry that his needs are demanding too much of the energy she needs to devote to a spouse, children, or career.

Third, we have a deep desire for truth as part of our finitude.[6] We long for coherence and understanding. We want our world to be intelligible; we want it to make sense. We search for answers and explanations. Problems have answers; puzzles have solutions. To be human is to be a meaning-making creature who uses reason to make sense out of the world. We do not live by instinct alone. We seek to discern meaning, order, and purpose in our interactions with the world around us. We long for a world that "makes sense." We want what Gary Gunderson calls *coherence.* "Simply put, coherence is a sense that life makes sense, that what happens is comprehensible, that events are not random, but, at least, somewhat predictable as a whole."[7] But illness disrupts our sense that the world is comprehensible. In

6. Dunlap, *Caring Cultures,* p. 193.
7. Gary Gunderson with Larry Pray, *Leading Causes of Life: Five Fundamentals to Change the Way You Live Your Life* (Nashville: Abingdon Press, 2009), p. 89.

some cases, we do not know what causes a disease. In other cases, we cannot understand why we have been struck with illness. The woman who miscarries a much-longed-for child cannot make sense of why she is unable to bring a pregnancy to term. The man who suffers a heart attack after taking great care to eat well and exercise cannot understand why his body betrays him. And the world makes no sense to anyone when a child is diagnosed with leukemia. Traffic accidents that leave us disabled, house fires that leave us disfigured, and natural disasters that maim and wound us also defy our sense that the world is rational. Illness can shatter our confidence in truth.

Illness, then, can disrupt our desire for safety, relationship, and truth. When we become ill, it brings about "a face-to-face confrontation with the fact that every day we are alive, we are limited, fragile, vulnerable."[8] Illness forces us to confront the tragic dimension of our creatureliness. And it is this tragic, painful dimension of our finitude and creatureliness that so often tempts us to try in vain to overcome it. So, while we must honor and embrace the goodness of our finitude, we must also confront its tragic elements honestly. We cannot deny the pain and suffering that sometimes accompany the limitations of our lives.

If healthcare must be intentional in respecting the goodness of our finitude and not trying to overcome it, then perhaps faith and religious institutions need to become more intentional in respecting the tragic elements of finitude that bring suffering. Too often, people of faith assume or are counseled that the painful and tragic elements of our creatureliness are forms of punishment from God that greater faithfulness can rescue them from. But finitude is not sin and neither is it a punishment for sin. Too often, people of faith are discouraged from naming and struggling honestly with tragedy and pain in churches and reli-

8. Dunlap, *Caring Cultures*, p. 11.

gious institutions. Too often the difficult task of cultivating the grace and spiritual maturity required for responding in healthy ways to the tragic dimensions of our creatureliness is eclipsed by well-intentioned and piously adorned forms of denial, blame, and promises of miraculous fixes.

In the face of tragedy, how are we to respond if not with pious denial, blame, or promises of miraculous fixes? The Bible, especially in the Psalms and the Book of Lamentations, offers us a different response, one that makes space for acknowledging the very real pain that accompanies our creatureliness.[9] In Lamentations, the prophet Jeremiah records his response to the horrors of the Babylonian siege of the city of Jerusalem. The residents of the city were starving to death; some had turned to cannibalism to survive; priests were slaughtered in the Temple. Jeremiah cried out, "Look, O LORD, and consider! To whom have you done this?" (Lam. 2:20). He cried out to God. On the cross Jesus offers a lament from Psalm 22: "My God, my God, why have you forsaken me?" (Mark 15:34). Both Jeremiah and Jesus ultimately hold God responsible for their suffering. Both are willing to shake their fists at God and show their anger, confusion, and frustration. Both trust in God's goodness and find peace even in the midst of a mystery they cannot comprehend. Lament does not end with anger, but neither does it bypass it.

Many people of faith feel awkward about raising a lament. It seems to fly in the face of everything we have learned about how to approach God with reverence and praise. It is time to learn again the full range of faithful, biblical responses to the life of faith, a life which is often wonderfully joyous, but sometimes painfully tragic. Learning to lament with Jeremiah, the Psalm-

9. Lament is also important for healthcare workers who witness pain and suffering on a daily basis. See Mary Molewyk Doornbos, Ruth Groenhout, and Kendra G. Hotz, *Transforming Care: A Christian Vision of Nursing Practice* (Grand Rapids: Eerdmans, 2005), pp. 34-37.

ists, and Jesus offers us a remedy to a superficial faith that demands that we meet every moment of life with a smile. Lament
gives us space to be honest about our pain and confusion in a
world that only praises those who show a brave face and to lay
that pain and confusion before God. It offers us a path toward
hope and peace that takes us straight through the "valley of the
shadow of death" (Ps. 23:4 KJV). Churches that offer ministries
of health and wellness must remember that part of that ministry
will consist of walking through that valley with those who suffer,
giving them permission and space to lament, and trusting that
God's goodness will ultimately prevail.

Coming Undone: Original Sin

Much of our bodily suffering arises from our limitations as creatures, and lament offers a helpful response to that suffering. But
not all of what goes wrong with our bodies is the result of being a
creature. Much of it arises from human sinfulness. Because we
are creatures, we return to dust. But sin is different. Sin is our undoing. Because we have come from God, if we turn from God we
have nowhere to go except back into the nothingness from which
we came. We should not, therefore, imagine that sin makes us
something other than what God intends. Rather, sin makes us
less than what God intends. In sin, we are coming undone. But
before we discuss the connection between sin and health, we
first need to be very clear about what we do and do not mean by
sin and about how health and sin are connected.

When most of us hear the words *sin* and *sinful,* we immediately think of the bad actions that we and others have done and
for which we are guilty. Or, we think of the actions we should
have pursued that we neglected. *Sin* and *sinfulness,* in other
words, refer to individual choices and behaviors that are dis-

pleasing to God and for which we should be judged. In the Christian tradition, sin has certainly encompassed bad acts, and there are times when those actions are directly related to our health. Engaging in risky behaviors can indeed lead directly to health problems. Eating highly processed foods can lead to obesity and diabetes. Smoking can result in lung cancer. Unprotected sex exposes individuals to the dangers of sexually transmitted diseases. A high-sodium diet contributes to hypertension. But there is a grave danger in connecting discussions about health and disease immediately to an understanding of sin as bad acts. It makes us likely to blame victims of disease for their condition. Fortunately, the Christian tradition has insisted on a more sophisticated understanding of sin, and this more nuanced view recognizes that sinful behaviors are manifestations of deeper patterns of brokenness and distortion in which we all participate.

The apostle Paul names the condition of brokenness and distortion *sarx*. In most English translations of the Bible, the Greek word *sarx* is translated as *flesh*. Before we can understand Paul's sophisticated view of sin, we first need to understand how he uses this word *sarx* so that it does not lead us astray. In the Letter to the Romans, Paul says that "to set the mind on the flesh [*sarx*] is death, but to set the mind on the Spirit is life and peace" (8:6). Throughout Romans, Paul consistently identifies *sarx* with life in sin and enjoins the Christian community to live according to the Spirit. Flesh, he argues, enslaves us, while Spirit sets us free. A casual reading might lead us to believe that Paul denies the goodness of the body. It certainly sounds as though he believes Christian life is bifurcated between a sinful body and a grace-filled spirit. Yet he also insists that Christians who have been united with Christ's death through baptism will also be bodily resurrected with Christ (6:5), and he likens the Christian community to the body of Christ (1 Cor. 12:12-27). Furthermore, he addresses the church at Rome as those who no longer live in the flesh *(sarx)* (Rom. 8:1-17). Now, clearly, the Roman Christians had bodies, so Paul must have meant by *sarx* something other than simply the bones and meat of the human body.

So, what does Paul mean by *sarx?*[10] Paul was deeply steeped in the traditions of the Old Testament. He affirmed with the entire Jewish community and with the earliest church that God had created the whole world, and that it was good. He also believed that human redemption included the body, which would be resurrected. Whenever Paul used the term *sarx* he spoke of a total human condition subject to the law of sin, a condition in which we are alienated from God and one another, a condition in which we do not even make sense to ourselves (Rom. 7:15). *Sarx,* then, does not mean a part of us, the bodily part. Instead it refers to an orientation, or rather a disorientation, *of the whole person.* Paul found a deep connection between our lives in *sarx* and idolatry. Every form of sin, that is, is ultimately an expression of lack of trust in God. Sinful actions emerge from a disordered, disoriented life that places ultimate value in something or someone other than God. This is a sentiment deeply rooted in the Jewish faith. The Ten Commandments begin with a prohibition on worshiping other gods because they recognize that lack of faith in God precedes and underlies every moral transgression. *Sarx,* then, refers to *the whole self* enslaved to sin, governed by deep patterns of brokenness, and living in the agony and chaos of a life not yet renewed by the good news.

Christian theologians have called these deeper patterns of

---

10. *Sarx* means many different things in Greek. It can mean simply "the body," the physical person, but in Paul's usage this is not what it indicates. Even in English the word *body* has this multivalent character. We can use the term *body* simply to mean to mean a person's physical features, but we can also use it to mean "whole person" as when we say, "Hey, everybody, I have some good news!"

brokenness *original sin.* Original sin does not mean the first bad act; it refers to the root of our sinfulness, the origin from which spring the myriad forms of distortion in our inner lives, in our relationships with others, in our participation in the natural world, and in our connection to God. Before sin is an act, it is a distorted orientation toward God and the world. Think, for instance, of Cain killing Abel, the first time the word *sin* is used in the Bible. Before Cain ever raises his hand against his brother, he first feels anger, rejects God's choice, and denies his fraternal bond with Abel. Before Adam and Eve reach out for the forbidden fruit or sink their teeth into the sumptuous knowledge it promises, they first have to want to be more than the limited creatures God made them to be. They have to want to be gods. Every action displeasing to God finds root in an underlying distortion in the human condition. The tragedy of sin is not so much that we act badly, but that we have lost our bearings as creatures who belong to God, creatures who live and move and have our being in God.

How do we become disoriented? Why did Cain reject God's choice? Why did Eve reach for the fruit? Why do we — each and every one of us — find ourselves in broken and distorted relationships? What is the origin of sin in human life? Part of the answer rests in remembering that while we are our bodies, we are also more than our bodies. We are creatures who think about and reflect on our own creatureliness. Unlike the earthworm, we are aware of our limitations, feel the tragedy associated with them, and can lament them. Finitude can be hard to bear for a creature who can think about its own creatureliness. We know that we "live and move and have our being" in God (Acts 17:28), and while this knowledge may comfort us, it also unsettles us. If my being is utterly dependent on God, then that means that I am not the cause of my own existence, the source of my own security, or the ultimate author of meaning in my life. Sin emerges when we meet the contingent nature of our existence not with trust, but with denial and self-deception.[11] Sin, as Paul and indeed the entire Old Testament affirm, grows where the human heart fails to honor God, where we place our final trust in something other than God, where we construct our own gods.

Original Sin and Health

Thinking of sin less in terms of personal actions and more in terms of the disorienting, deep-seated patterns of idolatry that lead our lives toward nothingness, brokenness, and confusion provides a helpful way of connecting *sin* and *health* and points to three practical considerations. First, thinking of sin in terms of pervasive patterns of brokenness in which our lives are caught frees us from the danger of blaming patients for their illnesses or stigmatizing them as especially sinful and undeserving of care. Even when we can draw a direct connection between personal actions or behaviors and disease, we must be very cautious about making moral judgments concerning the patient for two reasons.

On the one hand, we must be cautious with our judgments in that they tend to reduce a person's entire life to a particular bad action he or she has committed. In the final days of a struggle with emphysema, is the shop-owner who went out of his way to employ underprivileged youth for summer jobs, who was always generous at church with his time and resources, and who loved his family deeply just "a smoker" who deserves his disease? No. He is a full person, with a rich and complex life, a life that manifests both the deepest structures of sin and the profoundest

11. Reinhold Niebuhr describes the phenomenon in great detail in *The Nature and Destiny of Man,* vol. 1 (New York: Charles Scribner's Sons, 1941).

workings of grace. We should never make quick judgments about sin, disease, and a particular person because judgments about persons must always be judgments of their whole lives, and those judgments belong only to God.

On the other hand, we should exercise extreme caution when we make judgments about the relationship between sin and disease because of our own capacity for self-deception. Reducing sin to bad actions and focusing on the bad actions of others that we happen not to perform blinds us to our own caughtness in idolatrous patterns and distorted forms of living. Even if our own caughtness in the brokenness of original sin does not manifest itself in smoking, consuming too much alcohol, or eating an unhealthy diet, an honest examination of our own lives will inevitably disclose other forms of bad behaviors that may or may not be directly related to our health. Perhaps sin in our lives takes a form such as acquisitiveness or gossip that cannot be directly linked with poor health. But surely ill patients are no more guilty or undeserving of assistance because their actions contribute to disease than others are when their sinful choices do not. Self-righteousness has no place either in the church or the clinic, for in both places it inevitably involves self-deception and denial of one's own brokenness in ways that undermine the forgiving, good news of the gospel.

A second practical implication of thinking of sin in terms of our caughtness in patterns of brokenness relates to the educational dimension of healthcare. Education and instruction are a key element in the partnership between the healthcare provider and patient, and part of effective healthcare education involves cultivating self-awareness in patients so that they can begin to see, name, and develop strategies for discovering healthier, positive patterns to replace more destructive ones in their lives. A key part of healing patients involves cultivating in them a greater capacity to discern and reflect on the patterns of their lives and the relationship of these patterns to their overall health. When we reduce sin merely to bad actions and blame patients for them, we squander the opportunity to educate and empower them for healthy living. Empowering patients to discover their deepest life patterns and explore new possibilities is the way we meet sin with grace rather than with a shaming judgmentalism that contributes nothing to good health. Churches can be important partners in this educational process. Congregations that value and cultivate a culture where sin and grace are thought of in this more nuanced way prepare the hearts and minds of members for thinking more productively about their health.

A third connection between original sin and health draws us toward concrete strategies for acting on the insights that grow out of reflection. When we empower patients to reflect on the deep patterns of their lives and to imagine new possibilities, we must also provide resources and real opportunities for enacting such new possibilities. Encouraging individuals to exercise their agency for health and wellness only makes sense in a context where structures exist to make that exercise possible. This, in large measure, is what the Church Health Center strives to do in its Wellness Center. Patients in the clinic may be instructed in diabetes management, but in the Wellness Center they learn to prepare healthy meals in the teaching kitchen and find safe space to walk and exercise in the fitness center. The Church Health Center provides new structures that expand the capacity of its clients to exercise their agency. Churches and healthcare providers can become intentional in creating real, concrete opportunities for patients to act on and live out new patterns of life that promote well-being. Healthcare is not merely about disease control; it is about *wellness*. Attending to wellness means working to prevent the conditions that promote disease by cultivating healthy life patterns in patients. As much as healthcare providers must be attentive to wellness, so too must churches.

Churches can sponsor or host exercise classes, provide nutrition education classes, open their doors for health-screening clinics, and model good eating habits by serving healthy food at church functions to help members move from imagining new possibilities for their lives to enacting them.

Personal Sin: Two Ways of Coming Undone

Being attentive to these deeper structures of human sinfulness also has important implications for healthcare when we remember that the chaos and nothingness of original sin will be manifested in different ways for different people. In fact, the deep patterns of brokenness in original sin emerge in at least two complex and mutually aggravating forms of idolatry, sometimes as an excessive self-reliance in which we confuse ourselves with God and other times as despair. Understanding these two forms of brokenness is crucial for healthcare workers and for churches as they affirm the importance of the body.[12]

Excessive Self-Reliance

Looking out over the lectern of a seminary classroom on any given day, one is likely to see seminarians who are eager to learn so that they may better serve the church as pastors and church leaders. A growing number of these students are middle aged and completing one career while preparing for a second

12. For more on these two dimensions of sinfulness see Niebuhr, *The Nature and Destiny of Man,* vol. 1, pp. 178-207; Susan Nelson Dunfee, "The Sin of Hiding: A Feminist Critique of Reinhold Niebuhr's Account of the Sin of Pride," *Soundings* 65 (Fall 1982): 316-27; and Kendra G. Hotz and Matthew T. Mathews, "Fallen Religious Affections," in *Shaping the Christian Life: Worship and the Religious Affections* (Louisville: Westminster John Knox Press, 2006), pp. 33-44.

in church ministry. They have sacrificed much to enter seminary, and many are already serving in churches. However, a disproportionate number of such seminary students suffer from poor health or exhibit warning signs that they are headed toward poor heath. Many are obese, suffer from mobility issues, take medications for diabetes and hypertension, or show signs of heightened stress that is straining their bodies, spirits, and families. In informal conversations among students, one routinely hears that pastors and church leaders must put in long hours, or the work of the church won't get done. To be a successful pastor or church leader means sacrificing one's time and energy for the gospel even if it means compromising one's own well-being. Students also express concern that congregations often expect, reward, and reinforce this vision of the pastor. The pastor is expected to attend every gathering, to lead every initiative, and to be available on a moment's notice. Confronted with such pressures, students neglect the needs of their bodies, spirits, and families.

From the authors' field observation notes

The work of pastors and church leaders is surely important. Being present with the sick and dying, counseling those who plan to marry and those whose marriages are failing, educating children and adults in their faith, preparing sermons and prayers, coordinating outreach ministries, and attending endless meetings: these are just a few of the crucial works that pastors and church leaders undertake on a daily basis. Pastors and church leaders are often deeply committed to this work, sometimes at the expense of their own health.[13] They often find themselves re-

13. See, for instance, Rae Jean Proeschold-Bell and Sara LeGrand, "High Rates of Obesity and Chronic Disease among United Methodist Clergy," *Obe-*

warded for working endless hours in the care of their congregations; after all, they are doing God's work, and that demands putting aside other priorities in service of God.

Though pastors and church leaders are deeply faithful people, they suffer from sin and brokenness just like the rest of us. For many, what begins as a life of faithful service and commitment to God and the church subtly transforms itself into an unhealthy identity that comes to rely more on self than God. They are rewarded for an extreme form of self-reliance and often develop an acute sense that if they do not do the important work before them, it will not get done. Many find themselves building a lifestyle on the assumption that if they do not work as hard as they do, God's work will not get done. Put simply, many pastors and church leaders, with the best of intentions, begin to confuse themselves with God.

Pastors and church leaders, of course, are not alone in their tendency to rely on themselves at the expense of their reliance on God. They may be the most surprising example of our tendency to trust ourselves more than God, but they are in good company. We live in a society that rewards hard work and self-reliance and that teaches us that the only security we can know in life is that which we provide for ourselves. As a result, many of us come to confuse our professional status with our true identity.

This temptation to rely only on ourselves and to find our security in the work of our own hands is one way that original sin manifests itself in our lives. Sometimes sin finds its origin when we desperately seek to overcome our dependence on God and become utterly self-reliant. We seek to be the gods of our own lives. We try to stave off insecurity by accumulating wealth and power: we work long hours, neglect our family lives, and forget to eat

sity 18 (May 6, 2010): 4. Published online at http://www.nature.com/oby/journal/v18/n9/full/oby2010102a.html.

well and exercise. We strive for independence; we fail to invest our time and resources in building up our communities and instead spend our time immersed in "the good life," heedless of how our acquisitions come at the expense of others. We reject our finitude by idealizing youth; we mask our wrinkles with cosmetics and cosmetic surgery as quickly as they appear and cover our graying hair with dye. In committing this idolatry of the self, though, we can never truly succeed. We can never fully rule our own lives, never completely become independent. Because we live and move and have our being in God, we cannot flee God and make our home in some other reality, one fully under our control. Apart from God's life-giving presence there is nothing. There is no thing, no place, apart from God. And so, when we seek to become the gods of our own lives, when we flee God's reality, we can only come undone, returning through the mess of a chaotic life to the nothingness out of which God made us.

Sin that shows itself as a false form of self-reliance that refuses to recognize our limitations and dependence on God and other people affects our health just at it affects the health of seminary students and pastors. Seeking to be the gods of our own lives, even when it is concealed under service to God, can lead us to deny or neglect those places in our lives where we feel acutely our finitude and dependence. For the seminary students in our story, such excessive self-reliance serves as a powerful deterrent to seeking healthcare, and the resulting discomfort with and inattention to their own bodily needs and vulnerability exacts a steep toll.

Confusing professional status and true identity is one way that excessive self-reliance affects our health, but another important health dimension of excessive self-reliance relates to gender. There are few places where we feel more vulnerable and dependent than in the examination room of a clinic. Given the way our culture equates masculinity with self-reliance, it is not surprising that many men especially are reluctant to seek out medical care or engage in routine wellness exams. Faith communities need to explore and unmask the distorted ways that we construct our vision of masculinity and offer alternative understandings, ones rooted less in self-reliance and more in interdependence and mutual care. The gospel offers an alternative vision to a culture that teaches little boys not to cry and applauds the injured football player when he gets up from an injury and "walks it off" instead of seeking medical care. The gospel offers an alternative vision to a culture that encourages aggressiveness and competitiveness in the business and athletic worlds, and that, on television and in music and movies, valorizes violence among men as a legitimate way to resolve conflict. In the life and ministry of Jesus, we see a new vision of humanity that calls men and women alike to live in community, to share resources with one another, and to admit their needs and trust in others to meet them.

Naming excessive self-reliance as a form of sin should not lead us to blame pastors and other professionals who seek security in work or men who believe that seeking care is a sign of weakness. It should prompt us to address and offer alternatives to a set of social values that displaces God from the center of our lives and teaches us to rely only on ourselves. The point of understanding the structure of our sinfulness is not to cast blame but to find insight that might help us to turn toward being and away from nothingness, to seek God and abandon chaos. To do that, we need to uncover and address the deep structures of our sin.

Despair

I worked on a few "Plans to Get Healthy" during the evening. One child that I worked with was Vance, an 11-year-old who is severely overweight. We stepped outside the room to take his measurements, and after recording his weight he looked at me, nodding, and said, "Yeah, I know. It's weird." He said it so serenely, as if he just were acknowledging that he has brown eyes or is in fifth grade. We talked for a while after that about how weight is not something that makes you weird and how health is something you can work on improving no matter how old or what size you are. Vance, however, remained unconvinced.

From the field observation notes of Janelle Adams,
Rhodes College research fellow

"Sometimes I get dizzy, but I just sit down, and after a time it passes."
"Big momma had sugar, I'm a have it too."

From a conversation with
Congregational Health Promoters

Self-reliance is one way in which original sin manifests itself in our lives as individuals. This may be the primary form that original sin takes in the lives of those with some degree of social privilege and power. But there are other ways in which the brokenness of original sin may draw us away from God as the source of life and goodness. Sometimes sin emerges when the challenges of our limited lives become too much for us and we give in to despair, sinking into resignation and hopelessness. Rather than manipulating our world so that it conforms to our desires and convenience, we find ourselves trapped by circumstances so beyond our control that we almost embrace the chaotic swirl toward nothingness. Being more than a body, being able to reflect on our creatureliness, can become so burdensome that we prefer the simpler existence of the earthworm, the oblivion of not being an agent responsible for living into the image of God.

Despair is a form of idolatry because in despair we grant to the finite conditions of our lives the status of the sovereign God. We imagine that we are ultimately in their control, that they are the ultimate force in the universe that defines our lives, and that we are finally dependent upon them. Crushing poverty, domestic violence, and chronic unemployment cultivate resignation. "Knowing your place" as a person of color or a woman invites passive acceptance of one's position rather than an active embrace of one's vocation as a bearer of God's image. We see the signs of despair and hopelessness when young girls, desperate for approval and self-worth, become pregnant as teenagers; when young boys, desperate to be affirmed as men and to find companionship, join gangs; when the elderly, afraid of becoming a burden to others, lose their desire to live; and when people of faith, despairing of their ability to transform this world, abandon hope for this world and dream only of the next. We can come to experience so acutely our caughtness in forces and circumstances beyond our control that we give ourselves over to despair and resignation, and this too becomes an origin of sin.

The idea that original sin can manifest itself as despair has important implications for healthcare. Consider Vance's response, for instance, to his obesity. He sees himself as "weird," but also as helpless to change. Already at such a young age he finds himself caught in circumstances so far beyond his control that he cannot even imagine a different way of living. He cannot imagine being anything other than weird and seems resigned to a life defined by the taunts of children and the disapproving gaze of adults. Congregational Health Promoters report the same attitude of despair and resignation among members of their congregations. A woman at a health fair had her blood glucose measured. The reading came back very high, but when the Health Promoter offered her educational materials about managing diabetes she politely declined, saying, "Sometimes I get dizzy, but I just sit down, and after a time it passes." She accepted that her body would limit her, but not in the healthy way that grows out of accepting our finitude. She accepted the dizziness the way Vance accepted his obesity. Another Health Promoter reported that a pre-diabetic member of her congregation believed that developing the disease was inevitable. "Big momma had sugar," she explained, "I'm a have sugar too."

When you live in the midst of systems that operate over your head and structures that hedge your life in from every angle, what is the point of resistance? What is the point of exerting effort to make things different? When you are thoroughly defined as "weird," why strive for health? When all of your efforts yield no meaningful progress, when striving for goodness and beauty in your life always leads you back to the same dead end, when your best plans meet walls of resistance, then effort, striving, and planning can seem like a waste of energy. When the neighborhood has no grocery stores, farmers' markets, produce stands, or community gardens, when public transportation that could take you to those resources is expensive and inconvenient, then the energy it takes to find nutritious food exceeds the energy you could draw from that food. When the cost of buying nutritious food is more than you can afford, or the time to prepare it has been consumed by a second job, then the inexpensive calories of the nearby fast food restaurant or the candy bars of the convenience store begin to look appealing.

In medical contexts, this attitude is known as *fatalism,* and it can seriously hamper the ability of healthcare professionals to assist patients as they move toward health. Fatalism names a pervasive disposition that accepts ill health as inevitable, intractable, and irremediable. Fatalism grows out of a sense that the course of our lives is beyond our control and that illness, disease, and injury are to be accepted with stoic resignation. A patient who believes diabetes is inevitable sees little point in learning about how to prevent or manage the disease. A boy with no means available to make better food choices, who lives in a neighborhood where it is unsafe to exercise outside, remains unconvinced that any weight-reduction plan could be effective.

Here again, naming fatalism as a form of sin should not lead us to condemn persons who find themselves in despair. It should prompt us to remedy the conditions that produce hopelessness and fatalism. An observation we made about excessive self-reliance bears repeating: the point of understanding the structure of our sinfulness is not to cast blame, but to find insight that might help us to turn toward being and away from nothingness, to seek God and abandon chaos. To do that, we need to uncover and address the deep structures of our sin.

When we think about fatalism, some obvious causes and possible remedies present themselves. The challenges of poverty, public transportation, and food deserts are complex, but we can imagine ways to redress them. In fact, in the final chapter of this book we will describe in detail some communities and ministries that try to do just that. But beyond these admittedly difficult but obvious problems that might produce fatalism, there is another, much subtler source we need to consider: the church's own language about the bodily suffering of Christ.

Central to the Christian faith is the conviction that the bodily suffering of Christ won redemption for humanity. We speak of the unjust suffering that Christ endured for our sake. These truths are crucial to our faith, but sometimes we speak of them in a way that leads us to forget that Christ did not passively receive this unjust suffering. Jesus suffered beatings and mockery and bore the cross, we insist, and "never said a mumblin' word." But that is not quite right. Jesus did not quietly arrive in Jerusalem and lay himself down to be nailed on a cross. He preached a provocative message that threatened to overturn all the structures that ensured those with wealth and power would always dominate the poor and outcasts. He taught that "the last will be first, and the first will be last" (Matt. 20:16). He laid his hands on the ill and infirm and brought healing. The suffering Jesus endured was unjust, but not unexpected. His suffering was provocative, not passive.[14]

When we preach in such a way to suggest that Jesus suffered injustice passively, and that we ought to model our own response to suffering on his example, do we not suggest that injustices are to be endured rather than resisted? Such preaching, heard over the course of a lifetime, might reinforce an attitude of fatalism in those already disempowered, indicating that suffering is to be passively accepted and that illness is to be stoically endured. Our language about the suffering of Christ, in other words, may inadvertently serve as a source of fatalism.

This is not to suggest that we should change the gospel so that it conforms to our desire for good health. Rather, it is to remind us that a false gospel can damage our bodies. The true gospel does call us to suffer if working for justice brings it. The life of Christ does teach us not to flee to safety whenever the powers of the world threaten us. But Jesus does not teach fatalism, and the gospel is distorted when its liberating good news for the poor, the sick, and the outcast is turned into a call for them to accept their lot passively. The gospel rightly preached offers a powerful remedy for fatalism. It calls the church to work for justice so that structures of constraint are replaced by structures of opportunity and liberation. The gospel rightly preached calls us into provocative suffering that is the very antithesis of fatalism.

Attending to sin as a distorted orientation that can show it-

14. James Cone likens the cross to a lynching tree, which those with social power use to try to silence those who question the reigning hierarchy. Thinking about the cross as a lynching tree, he says, "can liberate the cross from the false pieties of well-meaning Christians." See James Cone, "Strange Fruit: The Cross and the Lynching Tree," *Harvard Divinity Bulletin* 35, no. 1 (Winter 2007): 53.

self differently in different lives is important in maintaining the sense of reciprocity and shared responsibility between patient and healthcare provider. For patients trapped in crushing poverty, unemployment, or deeply distorted webs of interpersonal relationships, achieving health can seem overwhelming. Despair and hopelessness can gnaw away at one's sense of self and undermine any sense of agency. Effective healthcare providers know that the path to good health includes empowering patients to invest in their own health. Effective healthcare providers work to cultivate partnerships in which they and patients share in developing strategies of care. Cultivating agency in patients requires acting with transparency, sharing information with patients, holding patients gently accountable by checking in on their progress toward wellness, and by creating time for patients to ask questions. Cultivating agency and overcoming fatalism will require healthcare workers to build trust with their patients.

"Something Else": The Social Structure of Our Sinfulness

Wednesday Luis could not have been more pleasant. He is a man who has sacrificed much for his family and yet seems content with the choice he has made. It is impossible for me to understand why he has had to lose so much. Three years ago his life was going well. He had a good job as an accountant in a small firm in Venezuela. He had recently bought a new home. His children were growing but his younger daughter, Gisela, became sick. She was only three years old. After a few tense weeks, she was diagnosed with leukemia.

One of the doctors who saw her knew of the program of St. Jude Children's Research Hospital in Memphis. There would be no cost to treat Gisela, and their success rate was very good. Without hesitating Luis packed the bags for the whole family and moved to Memphis. Within six weeks Gisela's cancer was in remission, but she would need to stay in Memphis for three years. The family's visas allowed them to stay as visitors, but they were not granted work permits. Within six months all of the family's savings were used up. Even though he does not have a permit, Luis went looking for a job and found work as a janitor at a local high school. He has held that job for the last two years.

I have seen him a couple of times since he came to Memphis and have learned many of the details of his story, which is very similar to so many of St. Jude's international patients. Today, Luis came to the clinic because he had hurt his back. He should be better soon, but wanted to be sure. He cannot afford to miss work. When I asked him about when he would return home, a big smile came over his face and he answered with one word: "January." Luis does not know if he will be able to get his old job back, but he is quick to say, "We have survived this ordeal; we can survive anything."

From the journal of Dr. Scott Morris

Clearly there is something wrong in this story. The wonderful work of healing Gisela free of cost stands in sharp contrast with her family's struggle. Her parents have no access to healthcare and no legal means of putting food on the table. There is something wrong here, and the wrongness suggests sin. We can sense the presence of sin saturating every detail of the story. But who is the sinner? Did Gisela commit some grave sin that caused her disease and set the wheels in motion for the whole tragedy? Did Luis sin by bringing his family to a top-quality medical center in the United States where his daughter could receive the care she needed? Did he sin in seeking work to provide for his family? Did his employer sin by providing it? Does the Church Health Center sin by providing healthcare to an undocumented worker? As soon as we ask them, we feel the nagging sense that these are the wrong questions. Something else is wrong here. Something bigger than one person, or even several people, making sinful choices is going on here. Something is wrong, indeed sinful, in a system that produces poverty for a family as a by-product of charitable healthcare work. Theologians name that "something else" social or institutional sin.

Often when we think of sin, we think of the way it manifests itself in individual lives. But as we have already seen, we are social beings whose lives and identities are shaped by the communities in which we live. Not surprisingly, then, we also find sin lodged in our communities' attitudes, habits, customs, and institutions. The same sinfulness that warps the patterns of the individual human heart gets woven into society's deep structures so that sinful patterns of action are perpetuated sometimes even without the intention of members of that society. Likely no one intended Luis and his family harm, but somehow the tangled structure of immigration laws, labor laws, the global distribution of healthcare resources, and the linkage of health insurance to employment in the United States produced a tragic set of circumstances that forced Luis to seek illegal employment so that he could provide care for his daughter and material support for his family. Though we may find a place or two in this story where individuals might have made different choices and produced a different outcome, it is very difficult to point the finger at any one person or choice and assign blame. That is because the sin in this story — and we should not hesitate to name it so — is sin of a different order. It is the sin of social and institutional structures.

One of the simplest ways to illustrate social and institutional sin in America is to consider the history of race relations. Think, for instance, of how housing discrimination on the basis of race,

59

which was perfectly legal throughout most of the twentieth century, affected zoning laws and lending practices. As the documentary *Unnatural Causes* explains, "between 1934 and 1962, less than 2% of $120 billion in government-backed home loans went to non-white households. In Northern California around the same time period, out of 350,000 federally guaranteed new home loans, fewer than one hundred went to Black families."[15] As white families, assisted by new loan programs, began to move out to the suburbs, businesses and churches moved with them. African Americans found themselves isolated in the poorest, least desirable neighborhoods, neighborhoods that had underfunded schools, poorly maintained infrastructure, and few banks or other financial institutions. Generations of children grew up with inadequate, outdated textbooks, with parents who were often forced by discriminatory hiring practices into low-paying jobs, and with little access to the corridors of political and economic power. Even today, when such discrimination is illegal and when one might be hard pressed to find a single overtly racist individual working in a local bank, we nevertheless find that African Americans are disproportionately denied housing loans or steered into so-called "subprime" loans even when they are well qualified for conventional mortgages.[16] Even today when segregation has officially ended, we find the legacy of generations of racism in the educational, economic, and health disparities that persist between black and white Americans. In other words, racism is a sin that negatively affects nearly every

15. "Place Matters" in the series *Unnatural Causes . . . Is Inequality Making Us Sick?* (San Francisco: California Newsreel, 2008), transcript p. 5. Published online at http://www.unnaturalcauses.org/episode_descriptions.php?page=5.

16. Harold L. Bunce, Debbie Gruenstein, et al., "Subprime Foreclosures: The Smoking Gun of Predatory Lending?" Published online at http://griequity.astraea.net/resources/industryandissues/financeandmicrofinance/predatorylending/subprimeforeclosures200602.pdf.

aspect of life for African Americans, and this is true regardless of whether individual people are themselves racist.

Using racism as an example, we can see the interlocking dynamics of social sin and institutional sin. First, we can see that sin pervades the social assumptions, habits, and customs of a community. The overt racism of an earlier age shaped the way people thought of and interacted with those of other races. Secondarily, this social sin became institutionally encoded in zoning laws, lending practices, and schools. Once sin is encoded in institutions such as government, business, schools, and churches it takes on a life of its own and persists even after significant progress has been made in rooting out sinful attitudes from the hearts of individuals. Even well intentioned people who work within the framework of institutions touched by such sin sometimes find themselves unwittingly and tragically perpetuating unjust practices.

This tangle of social and institutional sin has profound consequences for healthcare, explaining in large measure why health outcomes are so directly correlated with social circumstances. Researchers have confirmed that inequality and social injustice lead directly to poor health outcomes.[17] In the United States, there is a direct link between health and wealth that is not simply the result of the wealthy being able to afford better medical care. Disparities in health also emerge because inequality and injustice themselves produce conditions that lead to diseases such as hypertension, heart disease, and diabetes and that increase the incidences of infant mortality.

17. See, for instance, Brian Smedley, Adrienne Stith, and Alan Nelson, eds., *Unequal Treatment: Confronting Racial and Ethnic Disparities in Health Care* (Washington, DC: Institute of Medicine, The National Academies Press, 2003); Richard Wilkinson and Kate Pickett, *Spirit Level: Why Greater Equality Makes Societies Stronger* (New York: Bloomsbury Press, 2010); William Cockerham, *Social Causes of Health and Disease* (Malden, MA: Polity Press, 2007); and Michael Marmot, "The Social Pattern of Health and Disease," in *Health and Social Organizations,* ed. David Blane, Eric Brunner, and Richard Wilkinson (London: Routledge, 1996), pp. 42-70.

It is simple to understand how this happens if we imagine our distant ancestors hunting in the forest. They hear a roar and their hearts begin to pound. Our bodies are designed to respond to threats with a stress-response that helps us survive, the "fight-or-flight" instinct. When we confront a threat, "energy stores are released, our blood vessels constrict, clotting factors are released into the bloodstream, anticipating injury, and the heart and lungs work harder. Our senses and memory are enhanced and our immune system perks up."[18] This bodily response helps us to respond to an immediate threat and to survive it. When we hear the roar, we fight or run. But when the danger passes, our heart rate slows, and the stress hormones that had flooded our systems return to normal levels. But structural sin takes a natural and helpful response and warps it so that what was meant to protect us becomes the threat itself. Structural sin results in a social situation in which the threats never abate. The stresses of poverty and racism are relentless. The struggle to make ends meet, to provide the basic resources our families need, the constant sense that others regard us as inferior and that we and our children are denied opportunities because of it produces chronic stress. And when that happens the body's stress response ceases to be protective. A constant state of anxiety, accompanied by the body's natural stress response, wears the body down.

Conditions such as poverty and race that marginalize a person from access to social power produce chronic stress. Stress triggers bodily responses that wear away at our defenses and leave us vulnerable to disease. Whatever deprives us of the opportunity to shape our lives, to make choices in our own self-interest, and to have access to the power we need to enact those choices is likely to produce this stress response and increase our risk for disease. When we are deprived of the opportunity for

---

18. Wilkinson and Pickett, *Spirit Level,* p. 85.

companionship, a healthful environment, and meaningful work, we feel that our lives are out of control. When the structures of the world prevent us from the full expression of our agency, we become susceptible to disease. We are accustomed to thinking about biological causes of disease, but when faced with structural sin, we find that there are also *social determinants of health.* These social determinants produce disparities in health outcomes for people from different social classes. Poor people and members of racial minority communities, even when they make the best health choices they can, are still more likely to become sick and to die than are the socially privileged. The social determinants of health ensure that being poor does not mean simply that you cannot afford a luxury car or the latest gadgets; it also means that your health is compromised.

Structural Sin at Work: Neighborhood Disadvantage

> *All the resources we needed, my mother, my grandfather, my grandmother, my father, all got it right here [in the Hill]. I am amazed at that, because now you have to kind of shop around. If you want to turn your dollar over with your people, you've got to get a list and a map. But [back then] you could stay right here, and never leave it, and get everything you needed, from party-time to church. This is my memories of the Hill, was that families stayed together.*

> Lois Cain, a resident of the Hill District[19]

---

19. Terri Baltimore and Mindy Thompson Fullilove, "The Destruction of Aunt Ester's House: Faith, Health, and Healing in the African American Community," in *Faith, Health, and Healing in African American Life,* ed. Stephanie Y. Mitchem and Emilie M. Townes (Westport, CT: Praeger, 2008), p. 115.

Beyond the stress response, we find other ways in which social circumstances and healthcare are correlated, including what sociologists call *neighborhood disadvantage*.[20] Think back to the food desert. Living in such an environment clearly limits our choices for healthy, fresh food. Living in a neighborhood plagued by gang violence decreases the likelihood that we will take leisurely and healthful walks through our neighborhoods. Relying on inefficient and sometimes expensive public transportation makes what should be a routine trip to the market or doctor's office a cumbersome and time-consuming half-day journey. Working in low-wage jobs that do not offer health insurance makes it likely that we will not see a doctor for regular health checkups or a dentist for regular cleanings. Sicknesses that might have been avoided with regular health checkups may lead to missed work and make advancement in the workplace more difficult. Decaying teeth will lead to illness and affect our appearance and the way we present ourselves in job interviews. Poorer communities are more likely to be located near environmental hazards and to have older homes that have not been renovated to remove lead-based paint.[21] Needing to work multiple jobs to make ends meet leaves us with no leisure time or extra energy to strengthen our communities, to advocate for policy changes, or to court the business development that can revitalize a neighborhood. Poverty, in other words, works in multiple, interlocking ways to compromise our health and leave us vulnerable to disease.

The quotation at the beginning of this section comes from an essay entitled "The Destruction of Aunt Ester's House: Faith,

20. Kevin Fitzpatrick and Mark LaGory, *Unhealthy Places: The Ecology of Risk in the Urban Landscape* (New York: Routledge, 2000); Cockerham, *Social Causes,* pp. 149-66.

21. Dwight N. Hopkins, "Holistic Health and Healing: Environmental Racism and Ecological Justice," *Currents in Theology and Mission* 36, no. 1 (February 2009): 5-19.

Health, and Healing in the African American Community." It traces out a process that often leads to the destruction of poor but vibrant communities through the displacement of their residents. We see in the process a clear and troubling example of how structural sin works. We see in it that neighborhood disadvantage is no accident and that the poor health that follows is no surprise. Throughout the early twentieth century, racist attitudes and policies resulted in racially segregated neighborhoods. In spite of the segregation, within such neighborhoods a deep sense of community might develop and thrive. As the resident of the Hill explained, you could find in such a neighborhood everything you needed: family and friends, business and churches, recreation and work. Churches, community centers, and local businesses, together with residents who were invested in their neighborhoods, would work together to build a strong community. The residents might have been poor and the houses cramped and in various states of disrepair, but the life of the neighborhood could be vibrant.

A 1934 law, the National Housing Act, resulted in a practice called *redlining.* The Homeowners Loan Corporation, carrying out the imperatives of the new law, "created redlining maps for more than 200 cities. These maps rated neighborhoods on the age and integrity of the built environment, as well as the ethnicity of residents. Areas were graded A, B, C, or D. . . . Areas where blacks lived were given a D grade."[22] Residents of redlined neighborhoods were shut out from home-improvement loans, and businesses looking for new locations were unlikely to seek out D-rated neighborhoods. Soon blight would begin to settle in, and city governments would target blighted areas for "redevelopment." If a highway or stadium needed to be built, a redlined neighborhood was the first place to look. When an old, established neighborhood is razed and its residents displaced, the

22. Baltimore and Fullilove, "The Destruction of Aunt Ester's House," p. 115.

sense of community that once flourished is unlikely to survive. Without the network of streets, parks, and alleyways, without the familiar corner newsstand and the older residents sitting out on stoops watching the young at play, something of immense value is lost. Now "you've got to get a list and a map" to find what you need.

Living in a tight-knit community gives us a sense of home, a sense that we belong, and a sense of safety. That sense of safety and belonging is protective of our health. Residents of tight-knit neighborhoods, even if they are poor, can build trust and find a shared sense of purpose, which allows them to act effectively for the good of their community.[23] It is the stress of uncertainty, the anxiety of not having control, that wears away at our health, and this means that what happens in our neighborhoods is of first importance in what happens to our bodies. In the final chapter we will explore ways to address and overcome neighborhood disadvantage.

Structural Sin at Work: Unconscious Bias among Healthcare Workers

When you're talking about someone living 7 ½ or 8 years less just because of their race, that has to be addressed.[24]

Paula Jacobs, administrative director of quality
and patient affairs, Methodist Le Bonheur
Healthcare, North Campus

23. Sociologists call that sense of trust and common purpose *social capital* and argue that it results in *collective efficacy*. We will explore these ideas in more detail in the final chapter.

24. Tom Charlier, "Investigation at Memphis Hospital Finds Black Patients Suffer Care Gap: Disparity in Cardiac Case Treatment and Outcome," *The Commercial Appeal,* November 14, 2010.

Neighborhood disadvantage provides one example of how structural sin is at work in our world in ways that affect our health. Unconscious bias among healthcare workers is another. It is important to remember that structural sin perpetuates the damaging effects of sin even apart from the conscious sin of individuals. In fact, structural sin can damage our bodies even against the wishes of individuals. Healthcare workers — physicians, nurses, technicians, and so many others — devote their lives to the care of the ill and injured. They often choose their careers specifically because they want to help the less fortunate. Without question, healthcare work is a noble calling. But healthcare workers are also human beings, tainted by original sin and caught in sinful structures. It should come as no surprise, then, that even among those who believe in health equality, we find an unconscious bias at work that contributes to precisely the health disparities they wish to end. A study conducted at the north campus of Methodist Le Bonheur Healthcare system in Memphis, for instance, recently found disparities based on race in care of cardiac patients. The disparities showed up in how long patients were kept in the hospital, in how often they were readmitted, and in their odds of survival after a heart attack. These disparities persisted even when researchers controlled for factors like age.

In 2003 a study commissioned by Congress and conducted by the Institute of Medicine revealed just how deep and how damaging unconscious bias is. *Unequal Treatment: Confronting Racial and Ethnic Disparities in Health Care* showed that African American and Hispanic patients receive worse care in almost every sphere of medicine.[25] Augustus White, a professor of medical

25. Brian Smedley, Adrienne Stith, and Alan Nelson, eds., *Unequal Treatment: Confronting Racial and Ethnic Disparities in Health Care* (Washington, DC: Institute of Medicine, The National Academies Press, 2003).

education and orthopedic surgery at Harvard, summarizes their findings with respect to African Americans:

> Compared with whites, [blacks] had lower rates of cardiac surgeries, fewer hip and knee replacements, fewer kidney and liver transplants. Diabetic blacks were more often amputated than diabetic whites. Non-diabetic blacks were amputated more often too. Blacks were more likely to receive open surgeries rather than the less dangerous laproscopic procedures. Surgeons didn't operate on them as often for equally operable lung cancers. They received less pain medication for the same injuries and diseases. They were more likely to be castrated as a treatment for prostate cancer.[26]

Physicians do not say to themselves "this is a black patient, so I won't treat her well." Bias is rarely so simple or so obvious. But physicians and other healthcare workers do enter a patient's room with a set of assumptions about race that they have inherited from their culture. This is as true of black physicians as it is of white ones.

Augustus White considers bone breaks an example of how this bias operates. "A bone break," White explains, "is about as simple and straightforward as an injury can get. It has no relation to culture or language or unhealthy lifestyle, or whether African Americans might be averse to some kinds of treatments. It simply must be fixed, and the considerable pain of it has to be addressed."[27] But the *Unequal Treatment* study shows that even in the case of broken bones, black patients are less likely to re-

26. Augustus White, *Seeing Patients: Unconscious Bias in Health Care* (Cambridge, MA: Harvard University Press, 2011), p. 212.

27. White, *Seeing Patients,* p. 215.

ceive pain medication than white patients are. Why would this be the case? White speculates that physicians may operate with an unconscious assumption that black patients can endure pain better than white ones or that they are more likely to exaggerate pain in order to receive prescriptions for narcotics. He also notes that patients in pain are likely to be agitated and hostile. As a society, we have a strong aversion to black anger, especially to the anger of black men. Perhaps this very natural display of agitation and hostility in the midst of extreme pain is off-putting to physicians. Bias is not confined to physicians, of course; other healthcare workers will participate in the same social structures and share the same cultural assumptions.

Pointing out bias among healthcare workers should not lead us to blame them or to be self-righteous. We are all caught in the same sinful structures. Rather, understanding bias should lead us to increased self-awareness that can begin to address the biases we share and to overturn the structures that support them. Structural sin is complex, and our approach to it must therefore be sophisticated. The desire for self-awareness is precisely what led the Methodist Le Bonheur Healthcare system to conduct its study on disparity. The hospital did not try to hide its findings or justify them. Rather, hospital administrators revealed their findings publicly and worked within the community they serve to begin crafting institutional responses. Disparities cannot be addressed until they are found out. So long as bias hides in the shadows, health equality will be impossible to achieve.

The call for the church to care about bodies and for medicine to care about more than bodies means that we will have to contend with social and institutional sin. We cannot focus on personal sin alone if we are to live into the good creation God has made. If we are to build lives and communities that provide the healthful environment, meaningful work, and just relationships that God intended for us, then we will have to root out sin not only from our hearts but also from our societies and institutions. Healthcare workers will have to be attentive to the social dynamics that limit the healthful choices their patients can make and work to connect those patients with the social service agencies and churches that can help to remedy those conditions. Congregations will have to develop partnerships with government, healthcare organizations, and community organizations to make themselves more effective agents of change in their communities. Stewardship of the good bodies God has given us calls us to think big, to look for the "something else" that is going on when bodies break down, and to wrestle with the demons lodged in our institutions.

Thinking big should not discourage us, for big changes emerge from small actions. We may begin simply by inviting a nurse to accompany our pastors when they call on homebound members of the congregation. Area churches might cooperate to offer a weekly clinic or to arrange transportation for those who need to visit their doctor or dentist. A congregation may work to transform a vacant lot into a community garden that provides fresh fruits and vegetables to community members, builds a sense of pride of place, and helps to develop relationships among neighbors. Each congregation will need to discern prayerfully where God is leading it. Some actions will be easy and simple, others will call us to a more strenuous engagement with the powers of our world than we had thought possible. But the need to care for the body calls us to bring our full resources to bear on the challenges of social and institutional sin.

Conclusion

Throughout this chapter, we have explored the ways in which finitude and sin are related to health and disease. The biblical vision of human personhood indicates that we are finite and that our goodness, even the goodness of our bodies, has been corrupted by sin. We are limited creatures who came from dust and return to dust. These limitations are part of our goodness, but in their goodness, our limitations open us to the tragic. Although we cannot understand God's ways, we are free to lament the pain that sometimes accompanies our finitude, trusting that God accepts and redeems both our lament and our limitations. Our finitude opens us to sin when we pridefully reject our limitations with excessive self-reliance and seek to become our own gods and when, in despair and hopelessness, we kneel before the false gods of our circumstances. Our idolatry corrupts our whole orientation toward God and the world. Our idolatry produces bad actions, but more than that, it moves us into a spiraling cycle of chaos and brokenness, inviting us to consent to our own undoing. We see this tendency toward oblivion not only in our individual lives, but also in the lives of our communities and institutions. The call to care for the body, then, will call us to walk through dark valleys with those who suffer and to recognize and contend with the distortion in our hearts and in our societies.

Chapter Three

Redemption:
Our Bodies and Our World Remade

When most of us think of the personnel and equipment needed for a ministry of the church, we think about pastors and deacons, a pulpit and pews, a table and font. We imagine a church building designed for worship and filled with hymnals and Bibles. In Memphis, Tennessee, you can find a church just like that, St. John's United Methodist Church, on the corner of Peabody Avenue and Bellevue Boulevard. Directly across the street you will find yourself on the campus of the Church Health Center's clinic, and down the block you will find its Wellness Center campus. Both the clinic and the Wellness Center are ministries supported by St. John's and other local congregations, and the associate pastor of St. John's, Dr. Scott Morris, also serves as the medical director of the clinic. Here you'll find registered dieticians, physicians and nurses, social workers and wellness education coordinators. Here you'll find X-ray machines and syringes, treadmills and weight machines. Why would the church equip itself for ministry in this way? What have treadmills to do with hymnals? What have pulpits to do with blood pressure cuffs?

The answer is simple: faith and health, salvation and healing belong together. The church is concerned with faith, and clinics focus on health. The church is concerned with salvation, and clinics work on healing. We may be tempted to think of these as dichotomies, but they are not. If the church is concerned with faith and salvation, then it must also care for health and healing. And to the degree that the clinic cares for our health and healing, it also participates in our faith and salvation. As Gary Gunderson puts it, "faith needs the language of health in order to understand how it applies to life; health needs the language of faith in order to find its larger context, its meaning."[1] We are dust-and-breath creatures, the living image of God. We cannot care for the image and neglect the life any more than we can touch the dust and not honor the breath.

Remaking Our Bodies

We can see this link between faith and health most clearly if we look to the life and ministry of Jesus. Jesus came preaching the coming reign of God. He touched and healed the diseased. He ate and drank with sinners, forgiving them. And he taught all who had ears to hear. His proclamation of the coming reign of God encompassed healing, forgiveness, and education. He taught, he forgave, he healed, and all of these were signs of God's presence in our midst. For Jesus, salvation was all-inclusive. It brought healing to our minds, spirits, and bodies.

In the New Testament, a family of Greek words is used to describe redemption. *Sozein* is translated "to save," and *soteria* is translated "salvation." These terms can also mean "to heal" or "to restore" or "to make whole." This is because the Greek does not confine salvation to the soul. Whatever restores wholeness to the broken saves; whatever brings healing to the diseased con-

---

1. Gary Gunderson, *Deeply Woven Roots: Improving the Quality of Life in Your Community* (Minneapolis: Fortress Press, 1997), p. 4.

tributes to salvation. For Jesus, salvation was about this life and the next. It was about healing and wholeness here and now as much as it was about life everlasting. It was the triumph of grace in every last corner of a broken and wounded creation. Much popular American Christianity loses sight of this rich, comprehensive vision of salvation, reducing it to "going to heaven" after death. But this is a thin view of salvation that departs from Jesus' message in two ways. First, it pushes salvation entirely into the future, ignoring the calls for healing and reconciliation in our present world. Second, it confines salvation to our souls, forgetting that God has made and will redeem these good bodies.

To appreciate the intimate connection between faith and health we need to understand that Jesus taught a different good news from this thin, soul-only view. Jesus showed his disciples how God's reign was present already in their midst, and how that reign meant good news for all people. It meant good news for their bodies, not just their souls. God's reign meant that a few fishes and loaves could supply abundant food for a hungry crowd. It meant that diseases like skin diseases and mental illness that marginalized their victims would be healed. It meant that the poor would be raised up and honored. It meant that women and Gentiles would be included. The reign of God meant that the world was being set right even now. Jesus showed his disciples how to live in a world where God's reign had begun to grow like a seed in the ground, and that life included great enjoyment of the things of the body. In fact, Jesus was so often at table, enjoying good food and wine, good conversation and company, that his critics called him "a glutton and a drunkard" (Matt. 11:19). When God came into our midst, God became fully human, a dust-and-breath creature who slept when he was tired, ate when he was hungry, walked where he needed to go, died at the hands of a bloodthirsty empire, and rose again a glorified dust-and-breath creature.

Paul assured the church at Rome that because Jesus had

shared our dust-and-breath existence, we will share in his dust-and-breath resurrection. Paul's affirmation of our bodily resurrection is rooted in the reality of Christ's bodily resurrection. Because God has shared our human life, we may share in the life of God. Paul is confident that even as we have been made from dust and return to dust, we have also been made in the image of God and will be raised in that image. He leaves to the mystery of God what nature and form our bodies will take when God's reign is fully come, affirming only that *this* body will be glorified, taking on imperishability and immortality (1 Cor. 15). Like Christ, we will be resurrected bodily. Because we are our bodies, and because our bodies are subject to redemption, Paul reminds the church at Corinth that our bodies are the temple of the Holy Spirit and must be used to honor God (1 Cor. 6:19-20). What we do with our bodies and how we treat them matters.

Jesus and Paul both taught that grace embraces us body and soul. This grace transforms us not only in the next life, but also here and now. Grace reaches into all the places where original sin has twisted and distorted us and makes us new. Where we are coming undone, grace remakes us; and where we are returning to dust, it promises to breathe new life. Grace gives us hope where sin leads us to despair. Grace grants us the delight of interdependence where sin suggests that we can only rely on ourselves. Let's explore two stories of how grace transforms lives by overcoming despair and excessive self-reliance.

Rosie: The Grace of Self-Love Overcomes Despair

At the Church Health Center's Wellness Campus everyone knows Rosie. When she first arrived at the Wellness Center she weighed over 370 pounds and controlled her diabetes with 140 units of insulin a day. She had already lost 67 pounds on her own, but had done so with a crash diet, which was unsustainable. She felt that her only prospects were to continue to starve herself or die of diabetes, and she became depressed and suicidal. At the Wellness Center she began working with registered dietician Louise Jacobson, who taught her about healthy eating, attention to portion size, goal setting, and dealing with emotional eating. Rosie also began using many of the recipes provided by the Wellness Center and became an avid reader of food labels. She changed the way she shops and cooks. With the encouragement of the Wellness Center staff, she began attending a "Healthy Bodies" group led by wellness education coordinator Sharon Tagg. Now Rosie exercises regularly, continues to lose weight gradually, at a very sustainable one to two pounds per week, is down to 270 pounds, and uses only 10 units of insulin per day. Not only is Rosie's diabetes better, but she also suffers much less from a degenerative joint disorder and arthritis. Rosie is happiest because once her children began to notice the changes in her body and in their diet they wholeheartedly supported her. They thought her new dishes, like baked chicken instead of fried, were tastier than the old versions, and soon the whole family joined the Wellness Center. Soon Rosie and her children were all exercising while the grandchildren attended the Child Life Center where they learned about good snack choices. Small changes for one woman soon grew into a reorientation of an entire family's patterns.

Based on an account provided by Marvin Stockwell,
communications manager, Church Health Center

When we consider Rosie's story of health and healing in light of the biblical vision of salvation, we suddenly see how treadmills, dietary education, changes in shopping and cooking habits, and the mutual encouragement of one another toward good health are all dimensions of the good news of the gospel in her life and the lives of her children and grandchildren. Rosie's story is a story of salvation, a story of being restored to wholeness. While grace may certainly come in instantaneous, miraculous forms, as when Jesus touches the leper, it more commonly comes in more mundane, everyday forms. In a world which promises the false gospel of a quick fix, we must learn again the grace of the everyday, the power of God present in the ordinary. We walk on a treadmill and lose a pound or two a week; we successfully establish new routines for exercise; we shop, cook, and eat in healthier ways; we encourage and sustain one another with a hope that displaces despair; and we find that the journey toward wholeness of body also brings meaning, purpose, and delight to our souls. For Rosie and for most of us, grace does not come miraculously and in an effortless minute, but it comes nonetheless, and it does so gradually through the ordinary ministry of healthcare professionals, family, and friends. Salvation comes as baked rather than fried chicken; we read about this salvation on food labels; and like a mustard seed it starts small, perhaps claiming only one or two of our extra pounds a week, but before long it has grown into a new way of life.

Rosie's story tells us more than that salvation embraces the whole person and that grace often comes to us gradually and through everyday events, choices, and people. Rosie's story also points to a second important theological truth about health and wholeness, namely, that good health arises when human agency and healthy structures converge in our lives. Rosie's story is one of someone who chose to act differently. Rosie made a series of decisions to cook and eat differently, exercise more, and attend to the needs of her body in ways that she once had not. This took willpower and conviction, and Rosie should rightly take pride in the progress her better choices have made in bringing about her new degree of health and wholeness. It would have been easy for Rosie, faced with such severe health challenges, simply to lose herself in despair and give up on becoming healthier because the journey toward health seemed unachievable, exhausting, and impossible. As we have seen, such despair is often a manifestation of the brokenness of our fallen lives and involves a failure to recognize our value before God as those created in God's image and endowed with agency to shape important dimensions of our lives through our actions and choices. Rosie, however, refused to give in to the despair that is so tempting; she chose not to go down the path of medical fatalism. Rosie embraced the more difficult but rewarding path of better health. Part of the story of God's grace as evidenced in Rosie's life involves affirming that grace empowers us to act differently, to move from despair, fatalism, and resignation to new health and wholeness by embracing our agency as image-bearers of God.

Rosie's new choices and actions, however, did not occur in a vacuum. She was empowered to make better choices because she found herself in a new set of structures that enabled, supported, and rewarded those choices. Before Rosie could choose to shop for healthier foods and cook healthier meals, she needed to be educated about food labels, the nutritional benefits of healthier foods, and the health dangers created by highly processed foods. She also had to discover new recipes for preparing these healthier foods and be trained in how to shop and cook in a new way. Rosie also needed someone to educate her about the importance of exercise and someone to work with her, coaching her about how to exercise safely and most effectively. Rosie also needed a place where she could exercise safely and take advantage of well-maintained exercise equipment. Rosie surely needed encouragement, affirmation, and someone to hold her accountable in those moments when she was likely tempted to give up and fall back into despair and fatalism.

The Church Health Center provided a cluster of new structures that made Rosie's new choices possible and sustained her along her new path. Without educators to inform her about food labels and exercise, without cooking classes to train her to prepare new recipes, without wellness trainers to teach her how to use new and strange-looking exercise equipment, without healthcare professionals to help her learn to monitor her blood sugar levels, without safe buildings and equipment in which to carry out the day-in and day-out hard work involved in her choices, Rosie would likely never have been empowered to make the life-changing choices she has made. Rosie's choices did not occur in a vacuum; they occurred in the context of a new set of structures that enabled, supported, and rewarded her good choices. Such structures were essential in her journey out of despair and fatalism down the path of good health and wholeness. Rosie's story highlights the essential interplay of agency and structures. Before she could make the good choices she made, institutional structures had to be in place that enabled and sustained her as she made those good choices. Without such structures to support her choices, Rosie would likely not have chosen to live differently in the first place, or she would have given up once it became apparent that her choices had no chance at yielding success.

Finally, Rosie's story is not simply a story about improved bodily health. It is also a story of improved spiritual health. Her transformation involved not only losing weight, reducing her reliance on medications, and achieving greater mobility and energy. Rosie's transformation is also one of spirit. Rosie has come to love herself as a beloved child of God.[2] Rosie has come to see

2. Stephanie Mitchem makes a powerful case that "agency . . . stands against the internalized self-hatred found among some African Americans. Self-hatred becomes embedded into a group through its adoption of prevailing negative images." *Introducing Womanist Theology* (Maryknoll, NY: Orbis Books, 2005), p. 21.

and value herself differently. She has come to see and value herself as God sees and values her. As an image-bearer of a loving God, Rosie has learned to love herself, to embrace her goodness as a child of God, and see herself as one called by God to new life, health, and joy. Such healthy self-love is an essential part of Rosie's success. She has learned to love herself even amidst her brokenness just as God loves her amidst her brokenness, and it is out of that self-love that she found the energy to resist hopelessness, despair, and medical fatalism.

In one interview Rosie commented, "I'm enjoying Rosie now. I've never enjoyed Rosie before."[3] This graced love of self empowered her to carry on when carrying on seemed too much. This graced self-love, reinforced by healthy, life-giving structures, became an inoculation against all those viral forces, toxic habits, and paralyzing fears present both outside her and within her that told her that she was not worth saving and that her life was not worth living. Learning to love ourselves as God loves us is an important dimension of spiritual health, and in Rosie's case we see how such appropriate self-love both empowered her for bodily health and was in turn strengthened by the visible progress she made on the treadmill. But this should not surprise us, for we are dust-and-breath creatures whose spiritual health and bodily health are beautifully intertwined.

For some of us, talking about the value of self-love may seem awkward or even inappropriate. Quite often in the Christian tradition, we have identified sin exclusively with pride, or with an overestimation of our worth before God that is rooted in self-deification. Accordingly, Christians have sometimes identified all forms of self-love with selfishness and narcissism and held up the virtue of self-sacrificial love as the paragon of Christian morality. To be sure, original sin often shows itself as pride, self-

3. *The Early Show,* June 24, 2011.

deification, and selfishness. But as we saw in the last chapter, original sin can also show itself in our lives as despair, fatalism, and as a failure to value our own lives sufficiently. Most of us suffer from original sin in both of these forms in different moments and spheres of our lives, and our understanding of sin needs to be nuanced enough to help us name it differently when it shows itself differently. When we find ourselves claiming God's throne in pride, we do, indeed, need to hear of the importance of laying down our lives for our neighbor.

But when we find ourselves lost in original sin as despair, we need to hear again the importance of that graced kind of self-love, the kind in which we come to love and value ourselves as God loves and values us. Such graced self-love does not arise from selfishness rooted in declaring ourselves to be the gods of our lives; instead it arises from the liberating grace at the heart of the gospel that affirms that despite our brokenness and creatureliness, we are image-bearers of God who are still lovable to God. Before we are sinners, we are beloved image-bearers of God. This basic truth of Genesis lies at the heart of the gospel. It is out of the heart of the gospel, then, that we are called to a healthy self-regard that enables us neither to undervalue ourselves nor to confuse ourselves with God.

Rev. Terrell: The Grace of Interdependence Overcomes Excessive Self-Reliance

Reverend Earl Terrell, a successful pastor in Mississippi, has spent his life devoted to doing God's work. He has preached the gospel, served the sacraments, and provided effective pastoral care to his congregations. He woke up in the hospital after a triple bypass surgery and began reflecting on his health. He was a cancer survivor, diabetic, hypertensive, and

*suffering from congestive heart failure. He was also over-
weight. Reverend Terrell realized that he could no longer go
on living the way he had been. He realized that he needed to
take time to attend to his health, and with assistance from
the Church Health Center, he began to exercise regularly, eat
better, educate himself about diabetes, and visit his doctor
regularly to address his illnesses.*

From a conversation with
Congregational Health Promoters

Rev. Terrell's story is helpful because it allows us to see several
other important dimensions of the relationship between faith
and health from the perspective of redemption. If Rosie over-
came despair, then Rev. Terrell found the grace to overcome excessive self-reliance. Like many pastors and church leaders, Rev.
Terrell worked hard to minister to his congregation, and like
many of us, he worked long hours and set aside his own interests
to do the important work of God. But as he lay in a hospital bed
reflecting on his poor health, he realized that while the work he
was doing was indeed the important work of God, it was also killing him. Over the course of his ministry, he had gradually come
to believe that he was indispensable to the work of God, and for
this reason he neglected his own health as he ministered to others. In that hospital bed, Rev. Terrell came face-to-face with his
excessive self-reliance and discovered that it was the source of
his undoing.

Rev. Terrell's realization was a moment of grace in which he
rediscovered dependence on God and with it a sense of interdependence with other people. He discovered that by himself he
could not carry the entire burden associated with his work. He
rediscovered that he was a creature and not God, and that as a
creature his life was interwoven with the lives of others. He

learned that he needed to receive care as well as give it, and he learned that he needed to rely on God and other people to share the work of ministry so all might carry out that work in healthier ways. His rediscovery of the interdependent character of human life and the dependent nature of our creatureliness brought liberating grace that transformed his deepest perceptions of who he was and what it meant to be a pastor. Rev. Terrell's rediscovery of his interdependence with others and his dependence on God liberated him from that form of sin that we earlier identified as excessive self-reliance.

Rev. Terrell's story points us to two important theological insights that, while important for all of us, have a special relevance for pastors and church leaders. First, when we abandon excessive self-reliance and embrace the interdependent nature of being a creature, it sensitizes us to the need to honor the principle of sabbath and to engage in appropriate self-care. The principle of sabbath, rooted in the creation stories and the gospel, arises from the recognition that God created a world structured by rhythms and patterns, and that these rhythms and patterns include those of work and rest. To live out our creatureliness gracefully, we must learn to embrace the rhythm of work and rest that God has fashioned into the cosmos. When we observe a sabbath rest, we are intentionally taking time to be revitalized and to be made healthy and whole. For all of us, and especially for pastors and church leaders, taking time to observe sabbath regularly is essential to good health.

When we speak of sabbath rest, we should not understand *rest* always to mean utter inactivity, though surely rest encompasses periods of sleep and inactivity. Rest is broader than inactivity; it also refers to that constellation of leisure activities that bring refreshment and wholeness to our lives. Perhaps rest is a bike ride, a game of golf with friends, a picnic with family, watching a baseball game, or hiking a nature trail. Abandoning excessive self-reliance and recognizing the interdependent nature of our lives opens us to sabbath rest, and this in turn habituates us to be purposeful in our lives about engaging in the self-care necessary for good health. When we embrace the principle of sabbath and structure it into our lives and identities, we are engaging in a powerfully subversive enactment of the gospel. In a consumerist culture that rewards workaholism and reduces our identities to our work and earning power, pausing for sabbath routinely in our lives is a form of countercultural resistance to those forms of idolatry that urge us toward an excessive self-reliance where we confuse ourselves with God.

Second, when like Rev. Terrell we embrace the interdependent character of our lives, it transforms how we understand and undertake the work set before us. We learn to work in healthier ways. Here, too, there is a lesson for all of us, but for pastors and church leaders in particular. The biblical vision of the church is that of one body with many parts, of a community saved by one gospel but filled with diverse members with a variety of equally important gifts. The biblical vision of the church embraces our interdependence as creatures. When we live into this vision, we discover that pastors and church leaders do not carry the burden of God's work alone. The church — that diversely gifted body of believers — is charged with carrying forward God's work in the world. Rev. Terrell discovered that the work of God was not his alone but that of all God's people and that he could share that work with an empowered laity. Honoring the interdependence of the biblical vision of the church freed Rev. Terrell to embrace the principle of sabbath in a way that led down the path toward new health. The work of God is no one individual's alone. It is the work of the interdependent body of Christ. Pastoral work does not so much mean that we do the work of God for the people as it means that we empower the people to do God's work. Here is a more modest and much healthier vision of the calling of pastors and church leaders. For pastors and church leaders the road to good health often means abandoning excessive self-reliance and rediscovering the vision of the church as an interdependent community of companions in which all are called to God's work. Such a vision creates room for the healing power of sabbath in our lives.

Remaking Our World

The seed that starts small grows until it becomes a new way of life for individuals, but it also grows into a new world. We find a vision of this new world throughout the Bible, especially in the literature that biblical scholars call *apocalyptic.* Apocalyptic literature offers a vision of God's final triumph. Isaiah describes a time when the world is ruled by justice and peace, when cities are places of prosperity and delight, when violence is put to an end even in the natural world (Isa. 65:17-25). In Revelation, John envisions a city where the gates are never closed and where people from every corner of the world live together in harmony (Rev. 21). What prophets and visionaries throughout the Bible hope for and anticipate is the day when God's sovereignty and grace restore the whole creation. They envision not simply individual salvation, but the redemption of the entire social order and material world. In other words, apocalyptic literature describes the reversal of social and institutional sin and the establishment of justice and righteousness. No more will the insidious sins of past generations infect the institutions of the present. No more will "something else" warp and distort our best intentions. In John's vision of the city of God there is no temple because God's presence pervades every street and building, every home and school, every marketplace and museum. One need not go to church to find justice. In the city of God, justice is found in every human heart, but also in every human institution. The good we intend as individuals finds expression in the society we inhabit.

The apocalyptic vision of a redeemed order is expressed in the Old Testament by the Hebrew word *shalom,* which is usually translated *peace.* We often think of peace as the absence of conflict, and certainly it includes that, but shalom points to much more. Shalom means the presence of all the conditions that allow every creature to flourish. It begins where conflict ends and is not complete until the land, the people, and all creatures live together in health and harmony. In shalom, human flourishing does not come at the cost of the environment, and the flourishing of some does not come at the cost of the well-being of others. Instead, life is lived interdependently and in mutually enriching ways. We inhabit a healthy environment with clean air and water, engage in meaningful work, and enrich each other's lives through companionship. In shalom, all creatures give to and receive from one another that all may flourish. Attention is given to the comprehensive patterns of our lives and the way we depend upon and shape our total natural and social environment. If health is more than the absence of illness, then peace is more than the absence of conflict.

Apocalyptic literature, with its vision of shalom, does not offer us an idle hope that bids us to bemoan present circumstances while waiting idly for God to change them. Instead, it offers us a vision to guide our lives now. It offers us a template of God's plan for human lives and human society. Apocalyptic hopes compel us to renew our institutions even now, trusting in God to refine and complete our efforts in God's own time. This is why we find the earliest church not only preaching good news, but also continuing Jesus' healing ministry and collecting alms to support widows and orphans. The Book of Acts shows us Peter and the other apostles not simply sitting in an upper room waiting for Jesus to return, but actively reorganizing their communities so that wealth was not concentrated in the hands of a few, so that widows and orphans could find security, so that the diseased would be welcomed and healed, and so that the people of every race and nation could hear the good news and begin to renew their communities.

The biblical vision of shalom has profound implications for our bodily life in our present world. It reframes how we think about our individual bodies and spirits, highlighting how our daily lives are embedded in the natural and social environments. The apocalyptic hope for shalom prompts us to think broadly and to act systematically. It requires that we think about health and wellness in terms of the factors and features of our natural and social environments. The biblical vision of shalom carried by apocalyptic visionaries and prophets throughout Scripture calls us both to care for the health of individuals and to explore the natural and social factors that contribute to or detract from health.

Apocalyptic visions sustain us with the hope that God's reign is coming and prompt us to pursue shalom confident that God is acting even now. We always live in the tensions of a reign that has begun already, but that is not yet complete. We live in the meantime, in the times between the *already* and the *not yet*. Apocalyptic visions point us toward a complete shalom that is not yet fully realized and help us to see what is indeed already in our midst. Let's look at four places where we can see in the *already* a glimmer of what is *not yet*.

Churches "On the Move"

Koinonia Baptist Church knows how to heal people of their brokenness. Their church in Whitehaven, Mississippi, a suburb of Memphis, Tennessee, has an engaged and active health ministry that draws much of its inspiration from the Church Health Center. Their Congregational Health Promoters use the training from a free course provided by the Center to promote healthy living in their own communities. Each month the church focuses on a health issue or disparity, and the members of the congregation use the Center's resources to promote education about diabetes, provide blood pressure testing, or celebrate cancer survivors. They've been so successful that a member of their congregation, known in the community as "that sweet lady who does health ministry," joined the staff of the Church Health Center to encourage other congregations to seek health in their communities.

One of the church's most devoted Congregational Health Promoters is Cora Sue Smith. Four years ago, after she underwent triple bypass surgery, Cora Sue decided that it was time to take her health, and the health of her community, more seriously. She saw exercise not as something we did in our spare time, or even something that was a daily necessity. Rather, Cora Sue believed that exercising is something that is connected to our worship and praise of God.

Now, in addition to dress shoes and heels, spectacular crowns and suit jackets, the members of Koinonia Baptist Church bring their sneakers to church. On every fourth Sunday, Cora Sue leads the congregations outside after worship to walk. As a congregation, they walk around the community, and they walk as a community. She finds a way to make sure that every member of the community, even those with the most challenging physical and emotional difficulties, gets a chance to walk.

In addition to walking on Sundays, the members of the church are encouraged to walk [four] or [five] days out of the week, to wear a pedometer, and to track their health progress. Cora Sue encourages this extra participation — you never know when she is going to show up with incentives for the most improved walkers! But if you find yourself slowing down, Cora Sue meets you in worship and encourages you to get outside. Praising God through walking is her ministry, and is a part of a thriving and growing health ministry at Koinonia Baptist.

From the Church Health Center's
Ministry of Faith Community Outreach

Koinonia Baptist is a striking example, but it is not the only church with a growing and thriving health ministry. Over 800 people in Memphis alone have completed the same Congregational Health Promoter training that gave Cora Sue such inspiration. Churches are walking, cooking, serving, and praying, using the resources of the Church Health Center and the wisdom of their own communities of faith. This is not only occurring in churches whose neighborhoods lack traditional athletic spaces like local gyms or sports centers. Rather, churches with an array of resources realize that there is something important about walking in one's community, exercising at the church, or cooking meals in the context of faith.

In 2008, Sue Cleveland heard about a Church Health Center program called "On the Move in Congregations," and persuaded Germantown United Methodist Church to take up the program. "On the Move" is offered by the Church Health Center in conjunction with America On the Move in Tennessee, a health-oriented non-profit organization that aims to increase fitness. Staff members at the Church Health Center met with a small group from the congregation and trained them in how to use the program.[4]

4. The "On the Move" program was featured in a story by Kathy Culver in *The*

"On the Move" is a six-week program that encourages participants to interpret their health in terms of their faith. Participants receive a meditation journal with Scripture readings and reflections, a pedometer, and educational materials about diet and exercise. The journals focus either on the journeys of Abraham and Sarah or of Jesus and include maps of where they were likely to have walked. As participants record their daily steps in the journal, they imagine themselves journeying alongside Jesus. The program encourages participants to achieve three goals: to increase the number of steps they take by 2,000 steps per day, which is about a mile; to trim 100 calories off of their daily diets; and to consume three servings of low-fat dairy foods each day. For the first three days of the program, participants simply record their steps to determine what level of activity is normal for each person. After that, they work toward increasing their daily steps until they have met their goal. Members of the congregation meet regularly to discuss their journal reflections and to share their struggles and triumphs. They learn together about good food choices and how to incorporate more movement into their everyday lives.

The seed of God's reign is growing in the midst of Koinonia Baptist and Germantown United Methodist. It is not yet complete. Sometimes members make poor food choices, fail to support one another, drive when they could walk, or otherwise fall short of full health. And yet, we can see already in the midst of these congregations, in their very bodies, signs of God's redemptive love. First, Koinonia and Germantown are faithful to the biblical vision of salvation, which involves the whole person, body and soul. Their decision to start a health ministry was a direct and practical result of their theological commitment to the value

---

Commercial Appeal on September 15, 2008. http://www.commercialappeal.com/news/2008/sep/15/walk-this-way/.

of the whole human person, of their affirmation that God has made us breath and dust, and redeems us body and soul. Their confidence that the gospel is good news for our whole selves meant that they needed to address the ministries of the church to their bodies as well as to their minds. They needed preaching and singing, but also walking and eating. And they needed these things, the ministry of the soul and of the body, integrated.

Second, a holistic vision of redemption points to the need for integrated strategies of implementation. If in sin we are coming unraveled, then in grace God knits us back together again. In everyday, practical ways, grace addresses all of the dimensions of our brokenness — that of heads, hearts, and bodies. At Koinonia Church, we see grace at work in education that focuses on diet and exercise. In the creative use of the stories of Jesus and Abraham and Sarah, Germantown engages the minds and bodies of the congregation. In weekly gatherings to hold each other accountable and to offer mutual support, members develop new habits of the heart. And in moving their bodies, counting their steps, and choosing healthier foods, members' bodies are restored. In the integration of head, heart, and body, members' lives are transformed. They become living witnesses to the coming reign of God, and they bear in their bodies the promises of redemption.

Third, we see the "not yet" in the midst of the "already" in the way that Koinonia and Germantown embrace the universality of the church by drawing upon the resources of the broader body of Christ to strengthen their local ministry. God equips the church for its mission, but that "church," the body of Christ, does not exist solely in the local congregation. Every worshiping community participates in the church universal, the body of Christ. The idea of the universal body of Christ becomes real and practical when local congregations and denominations come together for shared ministries and to form networks for sharing resources. In these ecumenical, cooperative ventures, we see shalom growing in our midst. These churches need not invent a program to promote good health from scratch. They can adopt programming developed by others, adapting it for their own contexts. Each congregation need not aim for self-sufficiency, attempting to house all the resources necessary for every kind of ministry. Instead, the body of Christ flourishes when each community contributes what it can and draws from others what it needs.

Koinonia Baptist, Germantown United Methodist, and many other communities of faith affirm that body and soul are not two diverse realities, spiritual and physical, tethered to one another, or worse, at war with one another. Instead, their ministry acknowledges that as whole dust-and-breath creatures every inclination of the soul shapes the body, and every action of the body reverberates in the soul. We do not reflect as souls and walk as bodies. When we walk together, reflect on the journeys of Jesus, support one another's efforts, listen to a sermon, and choose whole, healthy foods, we do so as whole persons.

McMerton Garden: Genuine Peace Taking Root

At the corner of Merton Street and McAdoo Avenue in the Binghampton neighborhood of Memphis, Tennessee, uncared-for parking lots and vacant lots have been transformed into the McMerton Community Garden. Binghampton has many abandoned, boarded-up homes, rundown apartment buildings, and weeded-over vacant lots. Young people can often be found gathered on street corners, and gang tagging marks the landscape. Crime is a daily reality in Binghampton, as is the struggle for economic development and civic investment by its residents. In recent years, Binghampton has acquired a reputation as one of those neighborhoods that is best driven around rather than

92

through. In 2008, Binghampton was thrust into the media spotlight when a drug-related massacre of six members of a single family occurred in a house on one of its streets.

When Carl Awsumb and members of the Peacemakers class at Idlewild Presbyterian Church heard that many residents of Memphis were seeking to arm themselves for protection against the violence associated with neighborhoods such as Binghampton, they began looking for an alternative way to bring peace to troubled neighborhoods. They recognized that peace is more than the absence or suppression of violence. They knew that shalom required creating and cultivating the presence of the conditions of flourishing for the neighborhood, and they knew that one of those conditions was good health for its residents. They knew, too, that personal health was inextricably bound up with overcoming the entrenched patterns of social and institutional brokenness that marked everyday life in Binghampton. Perhaps if residents planted fruits and vegetables, genuine peace could take root.

Working together with residents of Binghampton, Awsumb and his fellow Peacemakers planted a community garden. The McMerton Community Garden has become a place where residents and volunteers cooperate to grow their own produce, and by doing so they come to know one another better as they work side by side planting, watering, weeding, and harvesting. Those who share in the work receive fresh fruits and vegetables from the garden at no charge. Children and young adults learn about gardening, develop gardening skills, take pride in the success of the garden, and come to invest in the revitalization of their community. As the garden has grown, its coordinators have developed partnerships with other community organizations that share its vision of shalom. For instance, at Caritas Village, a community center and restaurant situated at the heart of Binghampton in what was once an abandoned Masonic Temple, anyone can trade an hour of work in the garden for a nutritious meal, often made with produce harvested from the garden. Still more recently, the coordinators of McMerton Garden entered into partnership with GrowMemphis, an initiative associated with the Midsouth Peace and Justice Center. GrowMemphis promotes community gardens, recognizing that such gardens provide free or affordable produce in neighborhoods on the verge of becoming food deserts. Community gardening contributes to an overall improvement in the quality of life for those who participate, spurring neighborhood and community development, reawakening civic investment among residents, encouraging cross-cultural and intergenerational relationships that promote trust and goodwill among neighbors. Still further, community gardens create constructive alternatives of work and recreation to steer children and young people away from crime and gang activity. At the heart of the community garden movement is the insight that the health of our individual bodies and the health of our social bodies are inextricably bound together.

In McMerton Community Garden, we see already the presence of the coming reign of God breaking into the present. The mustard seed is growing right alongside tomatoes, squash, broccoli, and cabbage in the Binghampton neighborhood. The reign of God shows itself, first, in the way that the garden brings together the personal, the social, and the natural. The practice of planting the garden carries with it the affirmation that God is remaking our bodies, our communities, and our world. Redemption transforms our individual health, but also the health of our communities, and both of these are connected to the well-being of the land. Personal food choices are always embedded in social contexts that enable or inhibit good health. It does no good to teach people to eat fresh, whole foods if they have no access to those foods. Likewise, the health of our communities is ultimately rooted in the well-being of our planet. It does no good to plant seeds in polluted soil. A community garden systematically addresses the interlocking patterns of sin that undermine our personal health, the peace of our communities, and the beauty of our natural world. In doing so, community gardens participate in the apocalyptic vision of God's shalom.

Community gardens also point to God's coming reign because they embody justice rather than charity. Charity steps in to ameliorate the conditions of injustice and is a crucial part of the Christian mission, but Christian life also calls us to work toward establishing true justice and this is what community gardens aim to do. The McMerton Garden grew out of the vision and hopes of a small group of individuals, but from the beginning it was intentionally structured to promote grassroots participation, community investment, and sustainability. The garden intentionally, not incidentally, empowers neighbors. If it is not claimed by the community, then it will never achieve the broad social impact envisioned by its originators. Only when the residents themselves till the soil, plant the seeds, pull the weeds, and share in the harvest will the garden become a living reality in their imaginations and lives. Only then does it become a true garden of the community, rather than just a garden in the midst of their neighborhood. Only then does the garden become part of the vocation of the neighbors.

Community gardens also promote justice because they address many of the conditions that produce health-destroying stress. They bring together people of all races around a common task where all are equal. They break down the barriers of our class-stratified cities, bringing the possibility of making healthful food choices into every neighborhood. They produce open, green spaces where neighbors can meet each other without fear. Because they help to reduce crime, they ameliorate the stress of living in violent neighborhoods. They create opportunities for recreation and sabbath. In short, community gardens help to build order and to promote delight in new social structures that replace the old ones creaking under the weight of institutional sin.

We can also see the coming reign of God in the way that the McMerton Garden has grown in connection with a variety of community organizations, some of which are not explicitly religious. The idea for the garden began in a Sunday school class, but the faith of its founders was outward-looking, and its organizers have never resisted working with any person or organization that shared their vision for Binghampton. Being willing and eager to work with those who may not share our particular faith commitments is, in fact, part of our Christian faith commitment. When Christians affirm that God is creator and that God's reign is coming, we affirm that God made everything and that God is working to redeem the whole world. God works in and through the church, but not only there. God is active in every corner of the world, bringing peace in surprising ways and using every available agent and tool to establish justice. Christians, therefore, are those who have eyes to see and who are called to look for and embrace the work of God in the world wherever we find it.

St. Andrew African Methodist Episcopal Church: Seeking the Beloved Community

Are you expecting? Have you just become a new Mom and/or Dad?
If you are a first time Parent or Parent of many.
If you have given birth, adopted, or are expecting a child in 2011.
Come out and be blessed with a Baby Shower just for YOU!

From the website of St. Andrew
African Methodist Episcopal Church

Redemption

The St. Andrew African Methodist Episcopal Church website proudly announces the sixth annual Community Baby Shower. New and expectant parents from all over the city are invited to come and celebrate the blessings of parenthood. Like any baby shower, food is served, games are played, and gifts are given. But there is something different about this baby shower, for it offers gospel — good news — along with party favors. And there is also something different about this church: in a city with a tragically high infant mortality rate, St. Andrew aims to save not only souls, but also the tiny bodies of God's youngest children.

From the authors' field observation notes

In the heart of south Memphis, on the corner of the South Parkway and Mississippi Boulevard, stands St. Andrew African Methodist Episcopal Church, or "The Saint" as it is known in the community. South Memphis, like many urban neighborhoods, has not only a wealth of cultural resources and rich history but also a great number of community challenges that include poverty, crime, economic decline, and declining public health. As the members and pastors of The Saint looked around their neighborhood and city, they decided that God was calling them to minister to the needs of the community immediately surrounding them. Situated in a community with all the marks of the neighborhood disadvantage that compromises the health of its residents and with a pastor who holds an M.D. from Harvard and a co-pastor who holds a Master of Public Health degree from Yale,[5] it was clear that The Saint was well equipped to offer a unique healthcare ministry in its community.

---

5. Pastor Kenneth Robinson, M.Div., M.D.; Co-Pastor Marilynn Robinson, M.P.H.

Under the banner "Ministering to Memphis Spirit, Soul, and Body," The Saint has built a comprehensive and effective array of ministries to live out its vision of the gospel. In addition to the traditional activities one often finds at church, such as Bible study, choir practice, fellowship gatherings, and worship, one also finds ministries devoted to family enrichment, childcare, academic skills enhancement, economic development, and providing supplemental food and clothing to members of the community. In a program called DADS (Dedicated Against the Destruction of our Sons) men mentor boys, showing them that true masculinity does not require them to live as lone wolves, but instead beckons them to become connected to the community of God and to their families. But there is more. Amidst its wide array of ministries, The Saint has devoted itself to a variety of health-related ministries, including an abstinence program to encourage teenagers to reserve sexual intimacy for adulthood, a preventive health ministry open daily to the community, and aerobic and healthful living ministries. The facilities at The Saint include a Recreation and Retreat Center that houses a walking and jogging track, sports fields and courts, and exercise equipment. The Saint is also associated with a faith-based community housing development organization that has built affordable family housing in the neighborhood surrounding the church.

While one could easily single out any of its ministries, there is one ministry that is especially illuminative of the way that The Saint ministers to "spirit, soul, and body" in its community. Each year, through its LoveWorks Ministry, the Saint offers a community baby shower for its neighborhood and the entire Memphis community and invites all new and soon-to-be parents to this widely publicized event. Those who come to the baby shower receive a variety of gifts, including diapers, baby clothes, infant formula, bottles, blankets, and many of the other things needed to care for babies. But the baby shower is about more than providing these

helpful material resources. Present at the baby shower are re-
source people to help educate new parents and pregnant women
about the importance of prenatal care, good nutrition, childhood
vaccination, and pediatric healthcare. In addition to providing this
education, the baby shower serves as a place where new and pro-
spective mothers meet and establish relationships with healthcare
professionals and community organizations eager to assist them
with ensuring the best health for them and their babies.

In the last chapter, we saw how structural sin in the form of
neighborhood disadvantage can unravel the healthful environments we need for good health. As neighborhoods fall into economic decline, and institutions like banks, businesses, and even
churches begin to relocate to more desirable areas, a downward
spiral pulls residents toward worse and worse health. But a spiral
goes both ways.[6] If some small injury to the community can begin
the downward spiral, then by the grace of God, some small inter-
vention may begin to move a community back up again. Part of
the pain of sin is that it contaminates not only persons but also
whole structures. Likewise, much of the wonder of grace is that it
redeems not only individuals but also whole communities.

In the ministries of The Saint, we see the work of grace as it
draws mothers, fathers, and infants into an upward spiral of
hope and blessings. But we also see in these ministries the way
that grace heals structural sin, for there is a graced antidote to
the poison of neighborhood disadvantage. Sociologists call it *social capital* and *collective efficacy,* and Christian theologians,
most notably Martin Luther King Jr., name it *the beloved community.*[7] When he spoke of the beloved community, King envi-

6. Our thanks to the Rhodes College interns from RELS 460 (Spring 2011) for
this phrase.

7. King often used this phrase. See, for example, Martin Luther King Jr., "Fac-
ing the Challenge of a New Age," Address to the First Annual Institute on Non-
Violence and Social Change (Montgomery, 1956). Published online at http://

sioned a community bound together by love and in which every individual was valued, and where hope, peace, and justice prevailed. King also insisted that the beloved community was something that we could experience here and now. Through effective, peaceful action, the people of God could move their own neighborhoods, cities, and even their nation toward a fuller embodiment of the ideals of the beloved community.

Social capital and collective efficacy name two means by which neighborhoods and their residents might be nudged toward the beloved community. "Social capital," as William Cockerham explains it, "refers to a supportive social atmosphere in specific places where people look out for one another and interact positively with a sense of belonging."[8] This social capital is tremendously important for good health, and it is easy to see why when we recall that feelings of powerlessness, inequality, and isolation produce chronic anxiety that generates a stress response in our bodies. That stress response over time wears away at our bodies, producing health disparities. But just as isolation can make us feel threatened and therefore trigger a stress response, so also can a sense of belonging make us feel safe and therefore protect and promote good health. A sense of belonging protects individual health, but it can also transform a neighborhood through collective efficacy. "Collective efficacy theory emphasizes the capacity of neighborhoods to mobilize social action for positive outcomes," and studies have shown that residents of neighborhoods with high levels of collective efficacy have better health outcomes.[9]

What happens at The Saint when neighbors gather for a baby shower, then, is much more than a simple exchange of

mlk-kpp01.stanford.edu/primarydocuments/Vol3/3-Dec-1956_FacingtheChallenge.pdf.

8. William C. Cockerham, *Social Causes of Health and Disease* (Malden, MA: Polity Press, 2007), p. 167.

9. Cockerham, *Social Causes,* p. 178.

gifts and information. What happens is that connections are made and relationships are strengthened — social capital is built up and collective efficacy grows. As individuals find a place where they are accepted, a place where they belong, their chronic stress begins to abate, their bodies relax, and their health improves. Something as simple as a baby shower can begin to reverse the trends toward the low birth weights and infant mortality so often associated with the stresses of poverty. But the baby shower is not the only place where a sense of connection and belonging may grow. Many of the church's ministries promote health by reducing isolation and promoting belonging: Single mothers who might fear the judgment of the church are instead embraced and welcomed; boys find men who can offer them a strong model of how to be both compassionate and masculine; neighbors find safe places to walk. The more neighbors come to know and trust one another, the more they are rooting for each other, the more effective they become as advocates for their neighborhood. And through it all, the beloved community grows.

Congregational Health Promoters

"Oh, good," the woman ahead of me in line said when she spied the tables at the front of the room laden with healthy and delicious foods, "they're going to feed us." About twenty people gathered in a big meeting room at the Wellness Campus of the Church Health Center. By 6:00 p.m. sharp, everyone had signed in, collected a big three-ring binder, made a nametag, and found a seat at one of the tables. Most of us came straight from work — tired, hungry, and eager to learn. We had signed up for a class offered by the Church Health Center's office of Faith Community Outreach, and

we were there to become certified as Congregational Health Promoters. We agreed to meet for two hours every Tuesday evening for eight weeks. Every week speakers from the community came to share information with us and answer our questions. We heard from representatives from the Red Cross, from the American Cancer Society, from registered dieticians, and from just about every other community organization related to health that we could imagine. Classes covered nutrition, diabetes, hypertension, how to take medications correctly, prenatal and baby care, women's health issues, sexually transmitted diseases, mental health, and how to start a health ministry. We learned, laughed, questioned, and ate together, and by the end of our eight-week sojourn there were twenty Christians newly equipped to bring change to their congregations.

From the authors' field observation notes

"I got engrossed in that and, oh my gosh, here comes the story!"

From a conversation with
Congregational Health Promoters

Three times each year the Church Health Center issues a call for anyone interested in promoting health and wellness in their congregation to come for an eight-week training session to become certified as a Congregational Health Promoter (CHP). CHPs return to their congregations equipped with information and skills to begin new ministries, connected with a vast network of community resources to assist them in their work, and energized about the work that God is doing to renew humanity in body and soul. CHPs establish bulletin boards in their churches where they post newsletters, posters, and pamphlets about health. They organize health fairs where members of their congregation can have their cholesterol and blood glucose levels tested and where volunteer healthcare providers will take their blood pressure and talk with them about their medications. Some, like Cora Sue at Koinonia, establish walking ministries; others organize volunteers to relieve caregivers for Alzheimer's patients. The CHPs reach into their congregations and out into the neighborhoods in which those congregations are situated and ask, "Where is God working to bring hope and healing now?" They often start small, with just a bulletin board and a health fair, but once they get engrossed, "Oh my gosh, here comes the story!"

Nicole Gates, the Congregational Health Promoter with "the story!", is one of a number of perfectly ordinary Christians who has done extraordinary things with the training she received from the Church Health Center. Nicole currently serves as the coordinator for the Shelby County Infant Mortality Campaign. After her CHP training, where she learned about the appalling rate of infant mortality among the poor of Memphis, she joined forces with other women to start an infant mortality taskforce and a "Baby Safety Center." That work led her to the county taskforce, where she has received a national award for her work. Jenny Hutton, another CHP who also worked with Nicole on the infant mortality taskforce, now works with incarcerated teen girls to encourage them to develop healthy self-love, to cultivate habits that will promote good health, and to seek out healthcare rather than submit to fatalism.

Nicole, Jenny, and Cora Sue from Koinonia Church are just three of the hundreds of women and men who have received CHP training and who are using their gifts to discover what God is doing *already* in the midst of a world that does *not yet* fully manifest the reign of God. They are ordinary Christians from ordinary congregations who are doing the work of God, and their very ordinariness points us to an important theological truth. Ministry is not simply what happens when pastors preach and serve the sacraments. Ministry is the work of the whole body of Christ as it seeks to embody the values of the gospel and to enact the call of the gospel to preach, teach, and heal. The CHPs insist that healing ministries are just that, *ministries.* They are part and parcel of the work of the church, and not something tacked on as an afterthought. As ministers of the gospel, who focus on the redemption of the body, the CHPs embody what the Protestant Reformers meant by *the priesthood of all believers.*

The variety of ministries offered by CHPs points to another important theological truth about the nature of the church. On the one hand, the church as the body of Christ is one church. It is unified in spite of all of its differences. There may be many congregations, but the church is *one.* The Nicene Creed, one of the church's oldest doctrinal affirmations, says that the church is "one, holy, catholic, and apostolic." This means that the church is one wherever it exists (the term *catholic* means *universal*) and whenever it exists (the same Spirit that breathed life into the *apostolic* church is still at work today). It is the work of the whole church, then, to preach, teach, and heal. On the other hand, the church is also many. The body of Christ consists of many parts, and each part has a different role to play. Every congregation participates in the preaching, teaching, and healing work of the gospel, but each congregation will do that differently, in a way that fits with its distinctive character.

The Church Health Center does not provide CHPs with a cookie-cutter approach to healing ministries. Instead, it equips them with information and resources, and connects them to a vast network of others who care about health and healing. But staff at the Church Health Center also invite the CHPs to become partners in spreading the gospel of healing, and that requires them to use their intelligence and imagination to find ways to put those resources to work. Each promoter is embedded in a distinctive congregational setting, and each must seek out ways to promote health that are fitting to that context. "If healing ministries are to fully develop their potential to positively influence the health of individuals," Mary Chase-Ziolek explains, "they need to develop in a manner consistent with the culture of the congregations in which they are housed."[10] The community baby shower works so well at St. Andrew's because of the neighborhood in which the congregation is embedded. That same ministry may not work at all in another context. Cora Sue's walking ministry makes perfect sense for her congregation, but may fall flat in your own. A healing ministry must grow organically from the values of a congregation if it is to take root and grow from a small seed into a mighty bush.

Places like Koinonia Church, McMerton Community Garden, St. Andrew AME church, and the Congregational Health Promoter classes offer us a vision of what is possible as God's reign grows in our midst. The biblical vision of shalom, the apocalyptic hopes for a world remade, inspires the members of Koinonia and The Saint, the neighbors in Binghampton and the students in CHP classes to envision redemption for their bodies and souls; it prompts them to count their steps, plant their seeds, celebrate new births, and dream of transformation for their congregations. That same vision promises them that the seeds growing in their midst will someday mature into a majestic tree. Their faith has given them eyes to see what is growing in their midst, and their inspiring examples challenge us to ask, "Where is God at work in my community?"

10. Mary Chase-Ziolek, *Health, Healing, and Wholeness: Engaging Congregations in Ministries of Health* (Cleveland: Pilgrim Press, 2005), p. 4.

Invitation to the Table

Every Sunday, Christians around the world celebrate a simple feast. We come to tables laden only with bread and wine. The simple act of eating together — of eating and drinking whole, healthful foods — has always been at the heart of Christian worship. We gather as women and men, old and young from every compass point, from every race and social class. We come to have our bodies fed the simplest good things of the earth — the grains of the field and the fruit of the vine — and to have our souls fed the richest good things of heaven. We gather to remember what God in Christ has done for us, to receive undeserved grace that sustains us, and to refresh again the hope that emboldens us to act for peace and justice. This common meal is our way of enacting the apocalyptic vision. It is the place where, here and now, we live as though God's reign had already fully come. It is the place where everyone is invited and welcomed. It is the place where there is enough for all, where our bodies are fed and our imaginations fired. The table is the place where our Savior bids us come and rest, be fed and restored, and then go and re-create this table wherever we can and in whatever ways we can.

Consider your own community. Where is it most unlike the communion table? Where is the place to bring the bread and wine of God's good grace? Who is excluded from the table; who is not invited? Those are the people to bring in on important decisions. Where are the places where people do not have enough or do not have access to the simple, whole foods that sustain life? There is the place to set the banquet table. Since God has made us dust-and-breath creatures, and since sin is our undoing, we must look to the places where things are falling apart, returning to chaos and nothingness, and bring there the hope, justice, and peace that restore our bodies and refresh our souls.

Identifying the needs of our communities is the first step toward building a ministry of health and wholeness.[11] Perhaps there are many in your community who lack health insurance; perhaps there are many who lack access to real food; perhaps there are insufficient spaces or safety to encourage people to exercise. These needs can seem overwhelming, but simply looking into your world to see where the needs are is an empowering first step. Once you have identified the needs of your community, begin to educate yourself. Look for root causes, remembering that sin is complex and often lodged in social structures.

Next, remember that even the reign of God begins as a small mustard seed. When we begin to realize the systemic, structural problems that produce the conditions for poor health, we may despair of solving them. We may look to an organization like the Church Health Center and feel hopeless to establish something so comprehensive, but recall that even it began with a single doctor in an old house owned by a small congregation. So, start small. You need not do everything, but try to do something. Does your church have a parking lot that is not used most of the week? Could you make it available for a farmers' market? Do you have a vacant lot that might host a community garden? Might your members begin to count their steps? Do you have medical professionals who might organize a health-screening fair? In every corner of our world there are people struggling with incurable diseases who need someone to walk through the dark valley with them. Can your church provide training to members so that they can be present to share in the laments of those struggling with the tragedy of finitude? The ill and elderly often have caretakers who neglect their own health. Are there those who might volun-

11. For excellent practical suggestions on starting a healthcare ministry in your congregation see Deborah L. Patterson, *Health Ministries: A Primer for Clergy and Congregations* (Cleveland: Pilgrim Press, 2008) and *The Essential Parish Nurse: ABCs for Congregational Health Ministry* (Cleveland: Pilgrim Press, 2003); and Chase-Ziolek, *Health, Healing, and Wholeness.*

teer to share that burden so that caretakers can rest, exercise, and have time to restore their strength?

Once you have identified the needs in your community, educated yourself about root causes, and begun a small effort to meet those needs, then look around for partners. Who else is committed to health and wholeness? Remember that God often provides us with surprising companions. Noting the wildly diverse range of churches, synagogues, temples, mosques, and community organizations that support the Church Health Center, Dr. Morris has often remarked that people who could not agree on the price of a cup of coffee somehow come together to provide healthcare for the poor. We need not agree with others on every point of doctrine, moral matter, or political perspective in order to stand together to confront the tangled mess of circumstances that endanger our health and distort our bodies.

Look at your hands. Feel your pulse. Marvel at the workings of your mind. Know that you are dust made alive by the breath of God and sustained by the grace of God. The biblical vision of human personhood is as simple as dust and breath, as complex as original sin, and as satisfying as bread and wine. It is a vision that invites us to celebrate our goodness in all of its dimensions, to lament our tragedies, to repent of our brokenness, and to hope for and work toward the full restoration of every creature. Look again at your hands. To what cause will you put them?

Index

Adams, Janelle, 15, 18, 52

Agency: children's play and vocation, 20-21; and consumerist culture, 22; in a "food desert," 16; Genesis 1 and creation in the image of God, 6-7; and graced self-love, 77-81; and healthcare education, 45-46; and implications of despair and resignation, 57; and internalized self-hatred, 79n; interplay of structures and, 16, 22, 46-47, 77-79; nurturing patients' capacity for, 29, 45-47, 57; and sabbath rest, 25

Aging: changing bodies and changing identities, 9-10, 12-13, 19-20; story of ninety-two-year-old patient confronting, 32, 36, 37. *See also* Finitude and creatureliness

America on the Move (health-oriented non-profit organization), 89

Apocalyptic visions of a new world: the "already" and the "not yet," 87, 91-92; and the early church, 86-87; enacting through the common meal/communion table, 106; establishment of justice and righteousness, 85-87; Isaiah's, 85; John's vision of a city of God in Revelation, 85; as redemption of the entire world, 85-87; reversal of social and institutional sin, 85-87; vision of *shalom* and apocalyptic hopes, 86-87, 95, 105

Awsumb, Carl, 93

Babylonian creation account, 5-6

Baltimore, Terri, 63n, 65n

Beloved community, 99-100

Bible: apocalyptic visions of a new world, 85; Genesis 1 creation account, 5-8, 10, 23-24; Genesis 2 creation account, 3-5, 10, 13;

Cone, James, 56n

Congregational Health Promoters (CHPs), 26-27, 82, 88-89, 101-5; activities and healing ministries, 102-5; and biblical vision of shalom, 105; and the church as one/as many, 104; embodying the priesthood of all believers, 104; infant mortality taskforce and "Baby Safety Center," 103; ministry to whole persons, 26-27; and patients' despair and resignation, 51-54; training for certification, 26-27, 88, 89, 101-3; walking ministries, 87-92, 103, 105; work with incarcerated teen girls, 103

Consumerist culture: effect on individual and societal health, 22-23; as idolatry, 22; and social inequality, 23; as threat to sabbath rest, 25, 84; and vocation (meaningful work), 21-23

Creatureliness. *See* Finitude and creatureliness

Culver, Kathy, 89n

Despair and hopelessness: and church's language about Jesus' bodily suffering, 55-56; and cultivation of agency, 57, 77-79; and fatalism, 54-57, 78; how graced self-love overcomes, 75-81; implications for healthcare, 53-57; a patient's response to diabetes, 52, 53-55; a patient's response to obesity, 51-52, 53; as personal sin/idolatry, 51-57; un-

covering and addressing the deep structures of, 55-57

"The Destruction of Aunt Ester's House: Faith, Health, and Healing in the African American Community" (Baltimore and Fullilove), 63, 64-65

Diabetes, 52, 53-55

Doornbos, Mary Molewyk, 39n

Duke University Center for Health Policy, ix

Dunfee, Susan Nelson, 47n

Dunlap, Susan J., 35-37, 38; *Caring Cultures: How Congregations Respond to the Sick,* 35-37, 38

Enuma Elish, 5-6

Environment and health, 3-4, 14-17; and "food deserts," 16-17, 54; and Genesis 2 creation account, 3-4; healthcare that addresses, 15; "life choices" and "life chances," 16-17; poor communities, 63-66, 99; story of two sisters in the Child Life Program, 14-17. *See also* Neighborhood disadvantage

Faith: the link between health and, 73-85; and the tragic dimension of finitude, 38-39

Fatalism: and the church's language about Jesus' bodily suffering, 55-56; and despair, 54-57, 78; uncovering and addressing the deep structures of, 55-57

Finitude and creatureliness, 32-40, 71; being a body, 1-2, 8-10, 32-